FOR ALL THE SAINTS

RICHARD JACKSON

Published in 2021 by FeedARead.com Publishing

Copyright © The author as named on the book cover.

First Edition

The author has asserted their moral right under the Copyright, Designs and Patents Act, 1988, to be identified as the author of this work.

All Rights reserved. No part of this publication may be reproduced, copied, stored in a retrieval system, or transmitted, in any form or by any means, without the prior written consent of the copyright holder, nor be otherwise circulated in any form of binding or cover other than that in which it is published and without a similar condition being imposed on the subsequent purchaser.

A CIP catalogue record for this title is available from the British Library.

Front cover: The Garden Tomb, Jerusalem
                Artistic Impression: June 1997
                Mrs Phyl Boon (died 19/1/2019, aged 91)
                Bramhall Methodist Church Art Group

Back Cover: The Memorial Book,
                Bramhall Methodist Church

Table of Contents

FOR ALL THE SAINTS 1
RICHARD JACKSON.. 1
FOREWORD 8
BRAMHALL METHODIST CHURCH 9
REMEMBERING SOME OF THE SAINTS 15
   ARNOLD: Edward (Ted) died 9th January 1991 aged 80 15
   ASHTON: Stanley died 19th April 1994 aged 68 18
   ATKINSON: Norman C. died 10th Sept. 1992 aged 85.................. 20
   BEARDWELL: Helen died 1st July 1997 aged 92 22
   BEER: A. Gertrude died 5th December 1987 aged 83 25
   BOTHAMLEY: Kenneth F. died 16th Nov. 1993 aged 64 27
   BRITTON: G. H. (Bert) died 25th August 1995 aged 84................ 30
   BROOM: Geoff(rey) J. died 7th August 1996 aged 69 32
   BUCKLEY: Muriel(Mollie) died 3rd March 1996 aged 90 36
   BUTLER: Raymond G. died 24th May 1992 aged 71..................... 39
   BUTTERFIELD: Lily I. died 30th October 1994 aged 79 41
   CHESTER: Alice L. died 2nd March 1997 aged 76 44
   CLARK: Frank M. died 6th January 1996 aged 79 47
   COASE: Win died 2nd February 1995 aged 77................................ 50
   COOKE: George died 8th May 1995 aged 85 53
   CORRIE: Ellen (Nellie) died 31st May 1993 aged 100 55
   CORRIE: Freda died 4th February 1993 aged 69............................ 58
   CORRIE: Kenneth P. died 12th December 1991 aged 77 61
   DAVENPORT: Bryan M. died 18th March 1994 aged 52 63
   DENNIS: Daniel H. died 26th March 1994 aged 91 65
   EDWARDS: F. Margaret died 31st March 1994 aged 85 68

EVERARD: Hilda died 4th April 1994 aged 85 70
FEARNS: Hilda F. died 16th May 1988 aged 81 73
FLINT: Cyril died 11th August 1996 aged 63 75
HALFORD: Ian died 5th August 1994 aged 53 78
HALL: Gwynneth died 21st August 1992 aged 82 80
HARRIS: Margaret E. died 10th December 1993 aged 73 82
HINSLEY: Ida died 27th August 1994 aged 73 84
HORROBIN: James (Jim) died 20th Jan. 1996 aged 93 86
HOUGH: H. Marjorie died 5th June 1993 aged 76 89
JOHNSON: Anthony (Tony) died 12th Sept. 1994 aged 50 91
JONES: Edna M. died 11th July 1993 aged 72 93
LYON: Ruth died 25th September 1994 aged 79 95
McNEIL: Bessie M. died early December 1993 97
McQUILLAN: Alex(Zander) died 20th May 1996 aged 60 100
NEEDHAM: Bessie died 26th September 1988 aged 69 104
NEEDHAM: Norman died 2nd March 1994 aged 76 106
NICOL: Stanley I. R. died 22nd July 1992 aged 67 109
OVERALL: Sidney died 5th May 1993 aged 92 112
OWEN: Frank died 20th June 1996 aged 93 114
PARKER: Reginald died 30th July 1992 aged 66 117
PARKES: W. May died 11th November 1989 aged 85 121
ROBINSON: Harry H. died 18th May 1993 aged 71 123
ROTHWELL: Alma died 27th December 1995 aged 87 127
ROTHWELL: Arthur died 28th March 1993 aged 79 130
ROTHWELL: George died 12th February 1988 aged 80 133
SCURR: Frank died 8th September 1994 aged 79 135
SIMPSON: Mary died 3rd May 1994 aged 71 138

SLADE: Dora died 16th January 1993 aged 75 141
SMITH: Harold H. died 7th May 1994 aged 90 143
SMITH: Joan B. died 11th February 1989 aged 70 148
SOUTHERN: Winifred died 23rd Sept. 1996 aged 89 150
STUBBS: Kathleen (Kath) died 24th Sept. 1996 aged 81 152
TATTERSALL: May died 11th March 1994 aged 84 155
WENDT: Edna E. died 12th March 1998 aged 74 158
WENDT: Revd S Maurice died 24th June 1998 aged 76 162
WHARTON: Thomas (Tom) died 25th Dec. 1993 aged 96 166
WHITCHURCH: John F. died 22nd May 1992 aged 58 169
WROE: Rev'd John H. died 18th Jan. 1988 aged 76..................... 172
YOUNG: Sheila M. died 19th May 1995 aged 86......................... 174
MEMORIES OF OTHERS REMEMBERED 177
ALDRED: Leslie died aged 84 178
BARKER: Dorothy died 27th February 1988 aged 86 178
BARKER: Norman Cyril died 25th April 1988 aged 94 178
BARRIE: Denis St Clair died 2nd February 1991 aged 76............ 178
BLAND: June died 30th October 1994 aged 56 178
BRENNON: Harry died 1st June 1993 aged 60 179
BRIERS: Raymond U. died 31st July 1996 aged 82 179
BROWN: Mabel died 6th November 1990 aged 92 179
BURNEY: Mark died 25th September 1992 aged 91 179
BURNHAM: Lily died 3rd April 1991 aged 80 180
CASTELL: Jean died 20th May 1996 aged 82 180
COGHLAN: Robert (Bob) died 15th Sept. 1990 aged 82 180
COLBRAN: Richard (Dick) G. died 4th August 1996.................. 180
COOKE: Louise died 28th April 1992 aged 81 180

COOPER: Leslie died 2nd February 1990 aged 61 181
DUMBELL: Walter died 18th August 1995 aged 80 181
FORD: Vivienne (V.M.) died 25th June 1997 aged 89 181
GREEN: Maud died 1st December 1994 aged 94 181
HAIGH (HAY): Florence M. died 2nd Dec. 1992 aged 77 181
HALL: Muriel E. died 25th June 1988 aged 80 years 182
HALLWORTH: (Joe)seph died 14th Sept. 1989 aged 77 182
HARPER: Evelyn M. died 22nd November 1996 aged 85 182
HATTON: Kath(leen) died 20th August 1994 aged 73 183
HIGGINS: Sid(ney) died 12th February 1994 aged 72 183
HOBSON: Harry (Henry S.) died 1989 aged 88 183
JACOB: Rose A. died 9th January 1990 aged 75 183
KELLETT: Trevor J. died June 1997 aged 61 184
LAKE: William (Bill) H. died 26th Jan. 1997 aged 84 184
LAMB: Lily V. died 1st January 1991 aged 93 184
MATTISON: J. Leslie died 20th January 1991 184
MELLOR: Joe (Joseph) died 17th Feb. 1995 aged 79 184
NAYLOR: John E. died 27th June 1996 aged 65 185
NOBLE: Marjorie E. died 4th August 1989 aged 79 185
NORBURY: Anne died 27th October 1996 aged 87 185
PICKFORD: Ada died aged 89 185
POTTS: May died 6th June 1996 aged 88 186
ROBERTS: Peter J. died 25th June 1991 aged 62 186
SMITH: Lily died February 1996 aged 64 186
SOUTHERN: John L. B. died 26th April 1997 aged 61 186
SULLIVAN: John died 18th July 1990 aged 75 187
WARD: Annie (Nan) died 23rd April 1993 aged 92 187

 WHITE: Doris E. died 17th May 1988 aged 78 187
 WORTHINGTON: J. E.(Ted) died 3rd Apr. 1994 aged 72 187
 WRIGHT: Bertha died 28th January 1997 aged 89 188
SPEAKING PERSONALLY 189
POSTSCRIPT: A PERSONAL TESTIMONY 192
 DEATH ---THE LAST THING WE TALK ABOUT 192

FOREWORD

I was the minister responsible for Bramhall Methodist Church, one of the larger Methodist Churches in the United Kingdom from 1987 to 1997. This tribute to, **"All The Saints"** whose funerals I conducted during those years was prompted by the reminder that this year is the 150th Anniversary of the original church building in what was then the village of Bramhall. Mr Andrew Corrie is updating his helpful history of "Methodism In Bramhall" published on the 125th Anniversary, which prompted me to dig out from my own 'archives' much of what follows. On All Saints Sunday, 3rd November 1996, we shared in a service of dedication for our new "Book of Remembrance" documenting for the first time the Saints of the Bramhall Methodist Church. Unusually for a book of this kind, I am including an abbreviated outline of that service from 25 years ago because it provided much of the inspiration behind the publishing of this book today.

One of the great privileges of ministry within the life of the church is the opportunity given to us is to be alongside others at significant stages in their lives. Having said that, I will not be the first minister, nor the last, to say that it is only when someone dies and others share what they have known about that person that we really have a feel for what their lives have meant for countless other people in the church, the community and often the wider world.

Hopefully, what is shared in this book will be a snapshot of the kind of people who have helped to grow the Bramhall Methodist Church at the heart of a community that has been described as one of the friendliest in the whole of the country. The book will have served its purpose, if it reminds readers of the dedicated "Saints" in all churches for whom there are no statues, but who live on in the lives and communities that have been blessed through their commitment to the Lord Jesus Christ.

Richard Jackson (Revd Dr)

BRAMHALL METHODIST CHURCH
All Saints Sunday-3rd November 1996

PREPARATION with music for meditation

CALL TO WORSHIP-Jesus said, "I am telling you the truth: whoever hears my words and believes in him who sent me has eternal life. He will not be judged, but has already passed from death to life." John 4.24

HYMN 20 YE HOLY ANGELS BRIGHT,

INTRODUCING ALL SAINTS & THE DEDICATION OF "THE BOOK OF REMEMBRANCE"

Traditionally in the period around All Saints we are encouraged to reflect on the "Communion of Saints, the Forgiveness of Sins and the Life Everlasting". On this special occasion, I thought that we might find it helpful to reflect upon the lives and witness of some of the saints whose names are recorded in our Book of Remembrance. If I had the time, I've often thought that I would like to put together a book of my own entitled, "For All the Saints" which would gather together a variety of addresses given at Funeral Services down the years.

There is always human sadness associated with death, but that can be accentuated when people tip-toe around the bereaved and make it seem as though their loved one never really lived. I want us to make this service both a memorial to those who have gone before, including the Lord Jesus Christ, and a celebration of all of their lives. It's impossible to mention all the names of the saints recorded in our memorial book and some of you may be visitors or newer members, but I trust that your own book of remembrance will fill out what may be lacking for you in this act of worship.

Our son has a poster on his bedroom door- "If nobody is perfect, I must be nobody!". Indeed, nobody is perfect and I try to reflect upon that truth with a smile in a funeral service. "Ted Arnold was not everyone's idea of a saint", brought a few smiles and the odd nodding head in 1991, "He was strong minded and forceful. He could be dogmatic, stubborn and all those other labels that we attach to people who know their own mind. He crossed swords with many people in different situations and he did not suffer fools gladly." But I went on to say, "For whilst Ted was not a saint, he would have made a marvellous Old Testament prophet. The thing that held his life together was that he cared. He could not be lukewarm about anything because he cared about things with all the fervour of the prophets of old." Let's turn to page B5 of the service book, open our hearts to God, and in our confession admit to those things about us that cause heartache in other people-but let's question too whether those who upset us most do so because they are so like us in many ways.

B5–CONFESSION AND AFFIRMATION OF FORGIVENESS

Before the young people go out to their own groups, I just want to speak of one person in the Remembrance Book who had such a real love for children that he began teaching Sunday School at the age of 15 and became the Superintendent of four different Sunday Schools in his lifetime. You can look up the name of Harold Smith sometime. He devoted his life to the care of children and in 1950 became the "Children's Officer for the County of Staffordshire with responsibility for 1,100 children in care, a staff of over 300, 21 Residential Establishments including an Approved School, a Remand Home, and a training nursery for children's nurses." At Harold's funeral service in 1994 we sang a hymn that was first written for inclusion in a children's hymn book by a lady who is remembered for her Christian work among girls in West London. I think Harold would want to encourage all young people with the final verse of **HYMN 739**

MAY I RUN THE RACE BEFORE ME,
STRONG AND BRAVE TO FACE THE FOE
LOOKING ONLY UNTO JESUS
AS I ONWARD GO.

"The church and Circuit enjoyed the benefit of Kenneth Bothamley's considerable expertise as a Steward and Treasurer at Local and Circuit level." When we were discussing the future of the old church building it turned out that my dream of refurbishing was Ken's nightmare. In the church magazine, "he wrote pointedly and humorously of his own dream that fire engines were outside the church and the old building was completely gutted. It didn't stop Ken giving his wholehearted support to the Centrepoint project when it came into being and undertaking the treasurer's role for that project." Nevertheless, I think that the tribute most appreciated by the family was one that said, "To many people he would be known as a treasurer, but to me and my family, he was a real treasure."

THE OFFERING & DOXOLOGY

This evening, we shall be celebrating the work of Churches Together in Bramhall and the Covenanting Churches in particular. Our Church Steward, Zander McQuillan who died suddenly in May this year was Ecumenical in its broadest sense. Coming to us from the URC, with many friends at Ford's Lane, he helped to set up Christian Viewpoint for men and became Chairman of the Centrepoint Advisory Council. I said in its broadest sense because as we said of him, "Where others agonised about spending in the well-off churches, Zander made a personal commitment to his own church alongside that of needy churches like the Royal Thorn Evangelical Church in Wythenshawe and communities like Colshaw."

We are glad that Dorothy Boardman from the URC is with us this morning to read the Bramhall Covenant. The Covenant is all about Commitment to each other. It's quite often a particular scripture applied to a person that helps us to appreciate the commitment of a person who has died. It was a friend writing to express sympathy to the Rothwell family who suggested that the words of Micah 6.8 might have been written for Arthur Rothwell.

READING Micah 6.6-8

We were reminded of Arthur's strong sense of what was right by his traditional Methodist stance on Teetotalism and his active involvement in his Trade Union. I recalled his blunt comment to me at the door after a shorter sermon than usual, "Short measure this morning, wasn't it?" and my view that Louie, Arthur's wife, was the softener added to the hard water. But as I noted at the time the preacher in Arthur would have been repeating the first part of this text, "What doth the Lord require of thee? What doth the Lord require of thee?"

Earlier this week as I led the devotions for our Church Council, I read the story of Nathanael and was reminded of a member whom we likened to Nathanael. To quote. "I understand that I am not alone in thinking that Reg Parker was a most unlikely Police Inspector, for he was a man without guile. Somehow he served for thirty years in the Police Force without being tainted by the cynicism that sometimes affects those who have to cope with human behaviour at its worst."

Saddened by the death of our organist in 1993, I suggested then that you can only evoke memories of Harry Robinson who was, "A minister of music to everyone at times of significance in their family lives, baptisms, marriages and funerals and here in the regular worship of the church. Harry was as much called and dedicated to his ministry as any ordained minister." I've asked Sylvia Reindel with Edna's help to put together for us an organ medley that will remind us of Harry's contribution to the life of Bramhall Methodist Church.

ORGAN MEDLEY

Ken Corrie too was a one-time organist of this church. The Corrie family are part of the history of Bramhall, as well as of this church. Nellie lived till she was 100 in Hillbrook Grange. Ken her nephew died in 1991, and Freda his wife, who even with her walking stick, I described as "one of the fastest things on two legs, ever seen around the village of Bramhall". Freda, a long-time leader of the beginners used to say, "We have so much love for each other that there is plenty to spare for other people." Some talked of Peter Roberts, Stan Nicol and Freda Corrie running a Youth Club in heaven. Love to spare for young people they had in abundance. "Love to spare" would be an appropriate epitaph for all the people remembered in this book.

I turn to a minister now as representing the service of the whole church. The then Chairman of the District Ron Hoar, gave the address at the funeral service for John Wroe in January 1988 but I put together an obituary for the Minutes of Conference. That obituary was based on the following reading which epitomised John's life and ministry.

READING 1 JOHN 4.7-21   Pam Horrobin/Brian Couch

John Wroe's ministry to many was summed up in the words of one of his "youngsters" who came back for the funeral service. "He didn't preach at us - he loved us into the Kingdom of God and into becoming church members." Let's celebrate God's love brought into our lives as we sing:
HYMN 267 LOVE DIVINE ALL LOVES EXCELLING

DEDICATION OF MEMORIAL BOOK AND PRAYERS

HYMN 654 LORD OF THE LIVING,
   IN YOUR NAME ASSEMBLED

As we prepare ourselves for Holy Communion, I invite you to remember all of those of our Church Family who were sanctified in and through suffering. Stan Nicol's funeral service was linked together with a meditation on the three gardens of scripture. The Garden of Eden, symbolising those good things in our lives that God has planned for us and which give us great pleasure. The Garden of Gethsemane, is the place where all those suffering, their families and friends come with Jesus to the point of acceptance, "Abba, Father, all things are possible to thee; remove this cup from me; yet not what I will, but what thou wilt." The Garden of Eden, prepares us for the suffering and seeming separation of the Garden of Gethsemane, but the Garden of the Resurrection, is a glorious reminder that death does not have the final word, that those who have "fallen asleep" in Christ wake up with Christ. As I said of the three gardens in Stan's service, "Don't look for their location in a place, but in the faith that Stan had, that the God who gave us Eden, is with us in Gethsemane, and will continue to bless us in the Garden of Resurrection."

So, in preparing for Communion, I join the writer of Hebrews in Chapter 11:32 reminding his readers of the saints of old saying, "Should I go on? There isn't enough time for me to speak of Gideon, Barak, Samson, Jephthah, David, Samuel and the prophets." There isn't enough time this morning for me to speak of, Hodkinson, Grieve, and Flook; of Bates, Hinnem, Peters, and Ashton; of Barker, Fearns and Needham; Smith, Parkes and Brown; of Pearson, Atherton, Whalley, Whitchurch and Atkinson; of Overall, Hough, Wharton, Dennis, Ashton, Simpson, Richardson, Lyon and Bland; of Coase, Harrison, Young and Britton; of George and Alma Rothwell, Clark, Horrobin, Buckley, Potts, Davenport, Southern, Stubbs, Norbury and countless other people associated with this church, but as the writer goes on to say of all of them, "They did what was right and received what God had promised." The table is prepared for Communion. I invite you to remain seated for a moment in silent prayer praying for us, who share in offering communion, reflecting upon the Communion of Saints in heaven and on earth, and giving thanks for their lives. As it says in the letter to the Hebrews, "As for us we have this large crowd of witnesses around us". 12.1 You are then invited to come, whether church members or not, in a continuous flow to receive the bread and the wine in silence, and returning to your seats for meditation. After all have received, the organist will play the introduction and we shall join in our closing hymn. The Offering for Children in Need will be taken as we sing our final hymn.

HOLY COMMUNION

HYMN 814
FOR ALL THE SAINTS WHO FROM THEIR LABOURS REST,
WHO THEE BY FAITH BEFORE THE WORLD CONFESSED,
THY NAME, O JESUS, BE FOR EVER BLEST:
ALLELUIA, ALLELUIA!

THE BLESSING

REMEMBERING SOME OF THE SAINTS

ARNOLD: Edward (Ted) died 9th January 1991 aged 80

Ted Arnold was not everyone's idea of a Saint. He was strong-minded and forceful. He could be dogmatic, stubborn and all those other labels we attach to people who know their own mind. He crossed swords with many people in different situations and he did not suffer fools gladly. I'm told by many that he had mellowed by the time we came on the scene just over three years ago and I wonder how I would have coped with that forceful personality if I had met him in his younger days. I think it would have depended on how well I had come to know him. An unlikely Saint indeed!

For whilst Ted was not a Saint, he would have made a marvellous Old Testament prophet. The thing that held his life together was that he cared. He could not be lukewarm about anything because he cared about things with all the fervour of the prophets of old.

TED CARED ABOUT HIMSELF

That might seem a strange thing to say, but the determination that carried him through to recovery from strokes and ill-health in recent years was the same determination that has under-girded his life and work. Ted was a practical man who learned to love books. His practical training in engineering was augmented by further education found in books and after-work courses.

A determination to succeed brought him a well-earned B.A. degree and took him gradually through part-time lecturing from his career in the Co-operative statistics department into teaching and finally full-time lecturing at Kirby College.

TED CARED ABOUT HIS FAMILY

Married first to Rene who died so tragically in a car accident in 1970. Ted and Rene set patterns for family life that have stood David and Vivienne in good stead. No-one knows you quite as well as your own family. When a family love one another despite what they know about each other, it's a good sign. Ted's first words to Hilary at a University dinner in the early 1970's were so romantic they need to be quoted here, "Shall I pass you the potatoes?" This led to a second very happy and fulfilling marriage as they kept on passing the potatoes and Ted and the home's many guests carried on eating them.

The climax of such love and hospitality in their family life together came just before Christmas in the celebration of Ted's eightieth birthday. Ted was on top form and loved it. We are glad that Vivienne who sadly had to miss that celebration has been able to travel from Australia to share in this celebration of Ted's life.

TED CARED ABOUT PEOPLE

How little we really know about one another! Ted was a social person who loved to be among people. His involvement with the Sale Symphony Orchestra, the Manchester University Convocation, the Brookdale Centre and countless other organisations where he not only shared, but was willing to take on responsibility bear eloquent testimony to that fact.

There was also a private face to the man that was hidden from all except the closest friends and family. The man, who cared so much about one dyslexic student that they arranged to exchange letters weekly to help the youngster over his problems. The man who, with Rene his wife, agreed to forgo their 25th wedding anniversary celebrations so that they could pay for the wedding dress and the reception for a Nigerian student and his wife whom they had befriended. The man, who shared with both of his partners Rene and Hilary in offering something of the compassion of Christ to others.

TED CARED ABOUT THE CHURCH

From the age of seven when a stubborn youngster said no to a transfer from the Methodist to the Anglican Sunday School, Ted devoted his life to the Methodist Church. His turned-down offer for the Ministry of the church in his early twenties did not sour him with a feeling of rejection, but set him free to share his undoubted gifts in different ways through the life of the church.

His knockabout mimes to music at Carrington Lane Methodist Church belied the more serious man of the pulpit. The honorary chaplain of his RAF service days became the constant support of new local preachers in the church. Ted was an early enthusiast for the Ecumenical movement but he continued to be one who delighted in the worship and preaching of Methodism.

Nothing much needs to be said about the message of the gospel today. **The message is in the man. We thank God for what Jesus has done with a man who had many human flaws, but who showed us how to care about the things that really matter.**

An Amos in judgement, but with Hosea's love.

Thanks be to God!

ASHTON: Stanley died 19th April 1994 aged 68

A few years ago Stan Ashton gave me a copy of an American book that he and Shirley had found helpful in coping with the death of their son Mark. The book entitled, "Tracks of a Fellow Struggler" has a sub-heading, "How to Handle Grief". It is a Baptist minister's testimony of how he coped with the sickness and death of his 10-year-old daughter from acute leukaemia. Much of what I share with you today will be linked with thoughts from this book. John Claypool, the author, like so many preachers, turns in his thoughts to Job of the Old Testament when confronted by suffering and a loss that is hard to explain. He helpfully links the experience of Job with the prophetic words about Jesus Christ from Isaiah 53, "He was a man of sorrows, acquainted with grief." and points out that every experience of loss even in childhood is part of the process of us becoming "acquainted with grief."

Stan Ashton, like Job, had much for which he was thankful. From humble beginnings, he had done well in life as the world tends to judge things. A loving wife Shirley; a stable marriage of forty years; two much loved children in Mark and Tracey; later son-in-law Paul, and two treasured grand-children, Benjamin and Annie. A career as a design engineer that had taken him all over the world. A man of integrity who earned the respect of all with whom he worked. A contented man, with sufficient of the world's goods to anticipate a comfortable if not extravagant retirement, "He had it made."

The death of Mark at the age of 29 and later Shirley's illness could have brought anger and loss of faith in its wake, but it didn't. Yes, there was the shock, the numbness and some underlying anger in his oft-repeated, "When I get to heaven, I will have a lot of questions to ask" but, like Job, Stan was not questioning his faith, but wanting to ask questions of God because of his faith. Stan came to terms with the loss of Mark, because he had a life-time's experience of faith in God to draw upon. He brought to that tragic experience and his grief the same matter-of-fact faith and steadfastness with which he had lived the rest of his life.

Stan Ashton was a practical man who was seen at his best when he was involved in doing things. He could have stayed at home in his reserved occupation, but kept volunteering for the forces in the Second World War until he was accepted for the Fleet Air Arm. Brought up in the Anglican church and spotted for Methodism by Shirley from the choir seats of Eden Place Methodist Church, Stan used to say that you could not belong to the Methodist Church without having a job. How true for him! Stan was faithfully involved in everything from collection counting to youth work. The Friday night Threepenny Club, so-called because you paid one of those old twelve-sided threepenny bits to get in, which he ran in the late 60's with Rodney Searle and Bob Hamilton touched many young people at that time. Stan was not an up-front person but no-one, family, friend or in church, had to ask twice for his help with anything that he could put his hand to. For such a practical man he was also an extremely sensitive and emotional person who was easily moved. It was that sensitivity that reached out with the arm of comfort to touch more than one person in this church who had experienced bereavement. Stan knew how to weep with those who wept, but he always brought to people a genuine concern for them that helped to lift their spirits. He was a doer who cared. In recent days he organised everything from paper-work to shopping in ways that allowed him to continue to care for and share with Shirley in coping with her ill-health. It was a great joy for both Shirley and Stan when they were able to share in an Eastern Mediterranean cruise a couple of years ago. To visit Jerusalem together was one of those treasured memories that lives on and will help Shirley at this time to know the comfort of the "man of sorrows, acquainted with grief". John Claypool quotes the story of the father, whose son had died, asking the question of a minister, "Where was God when my son was killed?" and receiving the reply, "I guess, where he was while his boy was being killed." The mystery of undeserved suffering is focused in that death on the Cross. I think Stan, like the long-suffering Job, would want us to face the future with his triumphant words of faith ringing in our ears**,** "I know that my Redeemer lives." Job 19.25 **The questions, answered for Stan now, will have confirmed him in the faith in which he lived and died!**

ATKINSON: Norman C. died 10th Sept. 1992 aged 85

"LET NOT YOUR HEARTS BE TROUBLED; BELIEVE IN GOD BELIEVE ALSO IN ME." John 14.1

I suppose that this passage and this text in particular have given comfort to millions of people at times like this down the years. It communicates so powerfully because they are the words of Jesus spoken at a time when he knew that death was not far away and are addressed to a group of his closest friends who were distressed at the thought. Comfort is expressed in many different ways at the time of a death. Flowers, letters, cards, tributes of family and friends, and practical help offered are ways that people find to share in the loss of a loved one. All of these things have an impact on the feelings of those nearest and dearest in the short term. In the longer term it is our beliefs-our faith-that determines how we cope with death. Just last Monday I was being questioned by a non-churchgoer as to how those who belonged in the life of the church coped with the suffering and death of those whom they love. I was able to point to our faith, demonstrated in the lives of several within our own church who have been bereaved in recent months. It is what we believe about the one who said, "Let not your hearts be troubled", that influences how much credence we give to the promises of God shared with us in Christ.

LET NOT YOUR HEARTS BE TROUBLED ABOUT THE PAST. God offers us forgiveness for our past. Norman Atkinson had long been associated with the church and with this church in recent years, but it was in July that he was officially transferred into this fellowship. By that time, he was capable of little more than saying yes to becoming a member. He wasn't able to be with us in church on that day, but his pleasure at what had taken place was evident. His weakness at that time made his commitment the more real. As St. Paul puts it, "For when I am weak, then I am strong." It's then that we truly rest in God's promises. Forgiveness for you too! There are always regrets to be dealt with and we need to receive this same message for our comfort, "let not your hearts be troubled" about the past.

LET NOT YOUR HEARTS BE TROUBLED ABOUT THE PRESENT. We live in a troubled world and as I was saying earlier today at our morning prayers in this church, we need to remind ourselves that it is still God's world. Inevitably the problems of the present are heightened in the face of death. Emotions are mixed. The sense of relief that a person like Norman is no longer suffering can become an accusing dart in our own hearts. A new sense of freedom from the constraints of caring for someone throughout a long illness can be distorted by guilt feelings that would chain us to our loss for a life-time of sadness and mourning.

Jesus prepared his followers for their freedom and gave them the responsibility for sharing something of what he had shared with them. In some small way, all of us who have lost loved ones are entrusted with the responsibility for communicating what was good in their lives and our relationship with them to other people. As a long-time friend, that is what Donald Wilson has tried to share with us today. Your present is enhanced by what those who have died have shared with us in the past, but your present is enlivened by the presence of the one who has said let not your hearts be troubled. He promised also, "I will never leave you or forsake you."

LET NOT YOUR HEARTS BE TROUBLED ABOUT THE FUTURE The whole of this passage from John 14 bears testimony to the confidence that we can have in Christ. Good old Thomas questioned Jesus on behalf of us all, "How can we know the way?" Jesus responded: - I and I and I - It all rests with him. I have quoted before from this pulpit the words of Jim Elliot, a missionary who died young in South America. He said, "I don't know what the future holds, but I know who holds the future." Our Christian assurance at death rests in Him "who conquered death for us and opened the kingdom of heaven to all believers."

Jesus said, "Let not your hearts be troubled." about the past, present, or future. Norman Atkinson died in that faith.
We are called to live in it!

BEARDWELL: Helen died 1st July 1997 aged 92

Helen Beardwell could be a cantankerous old lady and by all accounts being cantankerous did not just come with old age. She was described to me by a former minister as, **"A definite personality of the old school".** Now that we know that we are all thinking about the same person and not pretending that Helen was some kind of plaster saint, we can reflect honestly on a life that gave so much dedicated service to her family, to the community and to the Methodist Church.

Helen was born in Greenock, Scotland, in an era when Britannia ruled. The British Empire occupied one fifth of the land surface of the globe and suffragettes were fighting for women's rights at home. She came to Birkenhead as the giant Cunard liner, Lusitania, was sailing from Liverpool to regain the fastest Atlantic crossing Blue Riband for Great Britain. Very different days that contributed to the growth and moulded the attitudes of this determined lady! Helen attended Primary School here in Tranmere, and the grammar school for girls in Birkenhead, before joining the workforce at Kodak in Liverpool. She married her childhood sweetheart Norman in 1929, set up home in Barnston and Bebington, before moving in 1939 to the present family home at 78 Cavendish Drive. A music-loving, dress-making mother with three children, Shirley, Derek and Martin filled the family home with fun despite the hardship endured as father went off to war leaving the family to cope with the Merseyside blitz and the shortages of war-time. Dad returned after the war to work at Lloyds Bank in Liverpool and the love and concern for each other shared in the family home laid the foundation of what was later to bear fruit in the lives of their children.

Christianity of the Methodist kind was caught rather than taught in the home as Norman and Helen's commitment to the Methodist church involved the whole family in that peculiar religious and social mix so much a part of the church in those days. To read a list of Helen's activities is to be presented with a historic cross-section of church and community outreach that had an impact on most aspects of this church's life. Support for Norman as Sunday School Superintendent, Church and Circuit Steward. Singing in the choir and at outside venues made her a natural for producing the children's spring concert at church. Home and Overseas mission interest combined with the fund-raising activities as Chairman of the Christmas Fayre.

Helen's involvement in the church Guild and the pastoral ministry of Church Flower Secretary did not preclude a wider service in Ecumenical activities as Treasurer of the World Day of Prayer and community concerns as founder member of the Forum Housing Association, Past President of the Birkenhead Girls' Secondary School Old Girls' Association, a member of the United Nations Association and so we could go on.....

For Helen, her Christian commitment was controlled by a sense of duty. There were things that one did as part of responsible living and things that one didn't do and there were not many grey areas in between. Like her children, Helen did get things done, even if feathers were ruffled in the process! I wondered where daughter, Shirley got that from!

That Helen could be actively involved to the end is down to her dogged determination and to the help given by family and her many friends, both inside and outside the church. Special tribute must be paid to her regular taxi-driver to church, Ken Isherwood, her caring neighbours at 76, Francis and Ursula, and the faithful Bill and Bob at 78 whose practical help morning and evening over many years made it possible for Helen to stay in her own home.

The family are glad that you are here today and hope that you will be able to respond to their invitation to join them after the service at the Cherry Orchard Restaurant, opposite the cemetery. They want to thank you for the messages of sympathy, and especially for the help you have given Helen in so many ways.

The deeply personal nature of Helen's faith is illustrated for us in the hymns that she chose for this service,
"In Heavenly Love Abiding" shares the serene confidence of the 23rd Psalm.
"O Love That Wilt Not Let Me Go" clings on to faith by an act of the will. "I rest my weary soul in thee: I give thee back the life I owe,"
For all her faults (and whoever is without fault, let him cast the first stone) Helen dedicated her life to giving back to God and to others something of what she had received.

It's true that Helen was born in the post Victorian era, but there was something of Queen Victoria about her. That famous enigmatic picture of Queen Victoria portrays her as a lady in black, saddened by the death of her beloved husband, dedicated to the service to which she was called and as a lady whose relations with those who were closest to her ranged from the affectionate to the stormy. I saw Helen last at Gerry's.?? birthday party - they don't talk about ages in this family! Despite her frailty Helen acted like royalty in the gathering, doing her duty, greeting people in that lovely voice of hers. A voice that survived the ravages of-doctor recommended-Craven "A" cigarettes in giving great pleasure to many through singing, and reading in places as diverse as Liverpool Cathedral and Bramhall Methodist Church. **The 'Queen' had her audience to the end! As with Queen Victoria, old age helped to mellow the person, just a little, and our memories today are fond ones.**

We give thanks to God for Helen, who could certainly be cantankerous at times, but who served God and others as a determined and dedicated lady of the **"Old School".** A little while ago someone said to one of our older members that she was like one of the "Spice Girls". She preened herself a little before the punch line was delivered- "Old Spice".

Helen will be one more saint to liven up heaven with a touch of "Old Spice".

BEER: A. Gertrude died 5th December 1987 aged 83

When I was talking with Gertrude in Stepping Hill Hospital recently, I discovered that one of her favourite hymns was "In Heavenly Love Abiding, no change my heart shall fear." It is one of the hymns chosen by the family for this funeral service and is one of the three great hymns of comfort all based on the much-loved 23rd Psalm. "The Lord's my Shepherd"; "The King of Love My Shepherd is"; and "In Heavenly Love Abiding" have helped comfort countless numbers of bereaved people down the years. The hymn was published in 1850 with the title "Safety In God" and is based particularly on verse 4 of Psalm 23, "Yea though I walk through the valley of the shadow of death, I will fear no evil, for thou art with me."

SAFETY IN GOD was something that Gertrude Beer had discovered for herself in her personal pilgrimage through life. I knew her for a few short weeks, but then many of us in the Bramhall Methodist Church knew her only in old age. Most of us did not know her during her early years spent married to her childhood sweetheart George. You would have had to ask questions, as I did, to discover more about those many years taken in bringing up a family; to discover the details about the Christian foundation laid in her home and family life and to discover more about the active service given to both church and community during many years.

The mid-sixties saw Gertrude and George move with their family to Chard in Somerset and join the Methodist Church there. 1972 saw Gertrude return to Bramhall on the death of her beloved George. Since then, Gertrude has been one of the regulars in worship and been part of the faithful members of the Tuesday Fellowship. As quite a private person, you would have had to ask questions of Gertrude to discover more about her personal life, but not about her quiet consistent faith. For by the time she had returned to Bramhall, her younger faith had matured into a deep assurance that there was and is "Safety in God".

Comments from family and friends alike, testify to her friendliness and her faithful Christian witness in every circumstance and situation.

That's why this hymn "In Heavenly Love Abiding" is so appropriate for this service. It begins and ends with that deep assurance of trust in God in and through every circumstance of life.

It talks about the present. About the storms of life that overtake but do not overwhelm us. We are given the picture of peace that is given to us in the heart of the storm, because we abide in God's love.

It talks about the immediate future. In whatever fears lie ahead we are reminded, "My Shepherd is beside me, and nothing can I lack." That God will be with us.

It talks about looking ahead to the longer-term future "which yet, I have not seen" and assures us with the promise that "He will walk with me!"

All through this hymn there runs a note of serene confidence in the Lord's unchanging love; this constant nearness; his watchful care; that makes the future bright with promise.

When we reflect on the life of Gertrude Beer and the way in which she faced death, we know that we have seen that serene confidence in the God of Heaven lived out on earth. No, Gertrude was not perfect, none of us are to the family and friends who know us best, but she was a lovely lady who lived out her life of faith in the one who loved her, Jesus Christ, her Lord and Saviour.

Having lived in friendship with Jesus in this life, she abides with him in death and all of us who share that faith can sing with assurance now:

> **"Thine be the glory,**
> **Risen, Conquering Son,**
> **Endless is the victory,**
> **Thou o'er death hast won."**

BOTHAMLEY: Kenneth F. died 16th Nov. 1993 aged 64

Kenneth Bothamley, as he was known to his family, was immaculate in dress, impeccable in manners, meticulous at work, a private person in many ways. Ken Bothamley, as he was known to his countless friends, a home handyman with woodwork and decorating, a walker, gardener, bowler, and cricket enthusiast, a season ticket holder at Manchester City, a Mancunian born and bred. What a contrast between the public image of the typical businessman and the man who came to church hoarse some Sundays because he had been so enthusiastic in his support of Manchester City at Maine Road on Saturday. In the few minutes that we have here I can only present a few snap-shots of what people saw in a life that was deeply rooted in those things that are unseen.

By training, aptitude and attitude an accountant, who eventually retired as Company Secretary of G.S.G., Kenneth Bothamley brought the best attributes of that profession to bear on every aspect of his work, church and family life. At work, Kenneth was painstaking in preparation and clarity itself in presentation. Nothing that Ken ever did seemed to be hurried yet he was rarely late for anything. Unlike many of us, he always seemed to have his mind in gear, before he began to speak. When he contributed to a discussion, you knew that it was a thought-through response to what had preceded it. He could feel strongly about something, but that strength of feeling was never out of control. The church enjoyed the benefit of his considerable expertise as a Steward and Treasurer at Local and Circuit level, but I like the comment of one person who said of Kenneth, "To many people he would be known as a treasurer, but to me and my family, he was a real treasure." It was his personal integrity and warmth that endeared him to people of all age groups. Few people have any idea of the time that Ken gave in providing personal, yes, I would call it pastoral help, to those who were struggling to sort out practical and financial problems in family life. We can only marvel at how much he fitted in when he was working, and thank God for what he has contributed in his so-called retirement.

Almost six years ago now, I had a dream of a refurbished building on what is now our Centrepoint site. My dream, it turned out was Ken's nightmare and he wrote pointedly and humorously of his own dream that fire engines were outside the church and the old building was completely gutted. It didn't stop Ken giving his wholehearted support to the Centrepoint project when it came into being and undertaking the advocate's role of treasurer for that project.

All of us will miss him, but his family will miss him most. Karen, Sally, Andrea and Paul had the privilege of being brought up in a home with a father who took family life seriously. Their memories are their own of home and holidays shared, of taxi services demonstrating that dad cared, but I think the description of how Kenneth took them out regularly on Saturday morning says so much about the nature of the man. The first visit was to the Post Office where they would sort out their own savings accounts. Then came the sweet shop! What a wonderful way to teach your children the lessons you have learned in your life.

Sheila became part of the family a brief eight years ago. She has loved and been loved and provided the Bramhall Methodist Church with one of its true romances as she and Kenneth grew emotionally, spiritually and physically closer together. Descriptions of their courtship here under the spotlight of the church's Romantic Review Body which they call the Church Council now, warm the heart. Kenneth and Sheila were meant to be together at this time in their lives and it showed. The children, partners and grandchildren have offered so much love to, and support for, each other during the past few years. Talk of Kenneth could continue and I am sure that it will outside the confines of this service as fresh discoveries are made of what he has meant to so many people in different ways. Personally, as his minister and a friend, I feel that he would want me to say something to help his family to cope with this second sudden death. First Beryl and now Kenneth. Now is not the time nor the place to reflect too deeply on our Christian response to death, but our personal feelings must be addressed.

The phrase that has kept coming to me is one linked with the promises made by parents in our baptism service. "Will you help him/her by your words, prayers and example to renounce all evil and to put his/her trust in Jesus Christ his/her Saviour." The response that parents make is, "with God's help we will". The promises were slightly different in earlier days, but the sense was the same. I think that Kenneth, by his words, prayers and example, has made it easier, not only for his children, but for others to renounce evil and put their trust in Jesus Christ. Worship, for Kenneth, was the focal point around which his whole life revolved. Intensely private in personal life and faith, he demonstrated the importance of worship for him by being here Sunday by Sunday. Discipleship, for Kenneth, meant discipline of self for the sake of others in work, church and family life. The pruned tree of Kenneth's life bore the fruit of Christ's Spirit in the love, joy, peace, patience, kindness, goodness, faithfulness, humility and self-control that he displayed.

Witness or example, for Kenneth, was the natural consequence of an ongoing relationship with the Lord Jesus Christ. Kenneth's words, prayers and example linger on, but he would want his children, his wife Sheila, his family and friends to be comforted by the words of the one to whom he looked for his example. Jesus said, "Let not your hearts be troubled; believe in God, believe also in me." Jesus said, "I will come again and will take you to myself, that where I am you may be also," Jesus said, "Peace I leave with you: my peace I give to you; not as the world gives do I give you. Let not your hearts be troubled, neither let them be afraid." You know, Kenneth was the only one who was really prepared for his death. Typically, all his church and business affairs were in order. The legacy of love reinforced by recent contact remains with the closest members of the family.

As Christmas approaches, we are reminded of a God who earthed his life in His Son born in a manger to show the world that God cares. God didn't stop caring when his Son died on the Cross. He entered into our pain and sadness. **It was faith in the Jesus Christ who lived, died and was raised again that sustained Kenneth in his life, may that same faith sustain you in his death**!

BRITTON: G. H. (Bert) died 25th August 1995 aged 84

Bramhall Methodist Church has many members and not everyone knows everyone else by name. When Bert took ill, people would sometimes ask me, "Which one is Bert Britton?" I would try to explain by saying that he was the tall, straight man who always sat with his wife Beatrice a third of the way down the church on the right-hand side of the middle aisle.

Yes, Bert was a tall man. Bert was the second of four sons brought up in the Richmond Hill Methodist Church in Leeds. His elder brother, who was engaged to be married, died suddenly at the age of 22. With a father who was often away from home, it was left to Bert to take responsibility for his mother, younger brothers and the bereaved fiancée. This experience helped to mould Bert's personality. Bert and Beatrice were married at Castleford her home town. She was not carried to church on the Ariel motor cycle which was to become their transport as they set up home at Crossgates in Leeds. Beatrice too was one of the few ladies around who stood tall enough metaphorically and physically to look Bert in the eye and theirs has been a happy marriage of like-minded souls.

Bert stood tall throughout his working life, working for the Co-op in Leeds, drafted into the Fire Service in Glasgow for the duration of the war and later moving with the Co-op on promotion to Manchester in the Flour Milling Department. Bert and Beatrice moved to Bramhall in 1955, joined the Methodist Church here and became a member of Probus as well as the Queensgate Bowling Club. Bert was twice made captain of the club as he proved his prowess in the game. Yes, Bert was a straight man. That straightness sometimes brought him into conflict with other people, but there was never any malice in thought, word or deed. Early in my ministry here I encouraged the congregation to sing the Lord's prayer on occasions. This brought a prompt and positive response from Bert who loved to sing the Lord's Prayer. We then began to sing it regularly on Communion Sunday, the first Sunday of the month. The problem was that if I changed the format or we didn't happen to sing it that Sunday I would be met at the door by a glare from Bert. "What happened to the singing of the Lord's Prayer, Richard?" Bert had a social awareness and a conscience that was sometimes a little difficult for people who didn't know him well to cope with. There were no shades of grey with Bert! Everything was either right or wrong and he credited others with the same strength of character that he himself had when discussing those rights and wrongs of everything from politics to religion. A self-made man himself, he found it difficult to come to terms with situations where others displayed weakness and a waywardness that was not part of his experience. Over the last few months people have seen much more of the true nature of Bert. **A good friend has called him a crusty apple pie. Crusty on the outside, but with a soft and sweet centre.** Tears came easily to Bert as he tried to cope with the problems that came to him and Beatrice in their old age. They were tears that had been there as he coped with other people's grief as a young man on the death of his brother. They were tears that had been there when his mother died during the war and as he supported her sister. They were tears that were in his heart for any person who was hurting. Perhaps for the first time in his life he allowed those tears to be shed for himself

Yes, Bert walked tall. Yes, Bert was straight. Yes, Bert was faithfully there in worship Sunday by Sunday. Did the naming of him after his mother's elder brother, the Rev Bertram Benn, have its influence. Certainly, he showed perseverance in getting to church one Sunday when he was staying at the Manse in Wrexham. Rev Benn did not drive, nor did Bert at that time, but he ended up driving the Rev Benn, Beatrice and himself to church in first gear and driving right round the church afterwards so that he didn't have to use the reverse gear. Nothing stopped Bert from getting to church! Bert could be cross with God at times, as he could be with other people, but towards the end he summed it up with, "God has been good to me." I think he would want to say now, "God has been good to me and so have you." Bert was thankful to God, thankful to Beatrice, and thankful to the family and friends who knew the soft and sweet man at the centre of the crusty apple pie.

Tall, straight and God's man. That will do him for an epitaph!

BROOM: Geoff(rey) J. died 7th August 1996 aged 69

As the family chose the hymns appropriate for this morning's service, they had to leave out one that they wanted. As I looked at that Hymn numbered 42, I thought that I might use it as a focus for our thoughts about Geoff and about God this morning.

> **O LOVE of God, how strong and true,**
> **Eternal and yet ever new;**
> **Uncomprehended and unbought,**
> **Beyond all knowledge and all thought!**

The opening of the hymn awakes within us a sense of wonder and praise as we reflect on the love of God. Geoff never lost that sense of wonder about God and about God's creation. As I sat at my small personal computer typing my notes for this address, I wondered what it must have been like for Geoff in those early days with Ferranti, working as an electronic engineer on that primitive computer that took up a whole room at Manchester University. Geoff often said that the pioneering computer required three rounds of the Te Deum before it was ready for action. There's a parable in that. The Te Deum, in praise of God, celebrating the genius of humanity. Gifted man that he was, the link was not lost on Geoff.

> **O heavenly love, how precious still,**
> **in days of weariness and ill,**
> **In nights of pain and helplessness,**
> **To heal, to comfort, and to bless.**

Geoff experienced life to the full. The army was in his blood. His father was in the regular army and you cannot be more army than to be born in Chatham, Kent. Younger days were spent in a very different Hong Kong to that which he was able to show Stella a couple of years ago.

Geoff entered the army at the age of 14 as a boy soldier at Arborfield Boys School and became a Staff Sergeant at the very young age of 19 when he returned to the school as an instructor. Early in 1952 Geoff was posted to Egypt at the time of the Suez Crisis. He worked on Centurion tanks and learned to drive in the desert. My notes say-"skills he passed on to his children." If you see a car being driven like a tank, it's Gillian in her new car.

The army, Ferranti, Computers, and the Sub Post Office. What was there in his earlier life that helped him cope as the days of weariness and ill quickly became nights of pain and helplessness. Geoff did more than cope! From that diagnosis a few short months ago, Geoff continued to deal with his illness in a positive way. Only family and close friends would have guessed how much pain he was in as he continued to make light of his illness and talk about the sports that had been so much part of his life. Football in the army, golf at Hazel Grove, winning two rifle competitions for Cheshire and in retirement the Church Bowling Club. He laughed as he talked about participating in that most dangerous of sports, mixed hockey with the gentle women of Bramhall Methodist Church. Dangerous sport indeed! Conversation with Geoff in hospital and home flowed in such a way that you hardly noticed the deterioration of body that left him so weak. It was in weakness that the love of God and the prayers of his many friends became so precious to him.

> **O wide-embracing, wondrous love,**
> **We read thee in the sky above;**
> **We read thee in the earth below,**
> **In seas that swell and streams that flow.**
>
> **We read thee best in him who came**
> **To bear for us the cross of shame,**
> **Sent by the Father from on high,**
> **Our life to live, our death to die.**

Geoff knew God as the "Great Architect of the Universe". He was blessed with the best human love could offer in his relationship with Stella from 1951. (Best man meets bridesmaid and marries her within twelve months!) Subsequently that same love was expressed in and through family life with Gillian, Ian and later his family, but he knew too that the only complete revelation of God was to be found in Jesus Christ. Whenever questions are asked about suffering and pain in the world, I am reminded of the Pastor's response to the parent who asked, "Where was God when my child died?" Gently he replied, "Just where he was when his Son died on a cross." Suffering is focussed in the Cross, but Salvation is too. Through suffering, Geoff came to understand.

> **We read thy power to bless and save**
> **E'en in the darkness of the grave;**
> **Still more in resurrection light**
> **We read the fullness of thy might.**

If a church funeral service leaves those who share in it thinking of the grave, it has failed in its purpose. Sadness, there will always be at death, but our Christian faith leads us through death into Resurrection.

That's why I am always pleased when the family, as today, choose a great Resurrection hymn to close the service on a confident note. In theological terms this hymn begins by celebrating the power of the Creator God, it continues by affirming the sacrificing love of the Saving God revealed in Jesus Christ, and it ends with the voice of human experience saying,

> **O love of God, our shield and stay**
> **Through all the perils of our way;**
> **Eternal love, in thee we rest,**
> **For ever safe, for ever blest!**

As the great Archbishop of Canterbury, William Temple pointed out, the essence of Christianity is not "God is love", but "God so loved that he gave".

Geoff too loved and gave so much to family, friends, neighbours and strangers. He was proud of the Minolta camera that he won in a photographic competition. Mocked by the family, he would say, "If you don't take part, you don't win the prize.".

Like the Apostle Paul, Geoff could have said at the end of his life,

"I run straight towards the goal in order to win the prize, which is God's call through Christ Jesus to the life above." Phil 3.14

That's the only prize that really matters.

Who says that you can only have three hymns at a funeral service?

Let's sing with and for Stella and the family:

Hymn 42

**O love of God, our shield and stay
Through all the perils of our way;
Eternal love, in thee we rest,
For ever safe, for ever blest!**

BUCKLEY: Muriel(Mollie) died 3rd March 1996 aged 90

Little Mollie Buckley has died. Most people used the word "little" not only to describe Mollie's stature, but also as a term of endearment describing someone much loved in this church. Mollie was not little in any other way.

Mollie may have been little as a baby born in Chorley to doting parents, George and Ada Buckley, on the 11th April 1905, and she was certainly tiny when she fell asleep in the Methodist Minister's pew (those were the days!) on Mrs. Henderson's muff. It was soon discovered that she had a great talent for music and a sense of humour.

As a young girl singing the solo part of a bee in the choir on the Church Anniversary, she said, "I'm not nervous because I pretend I'm in a field of cabbages." Her confidence led to her becoming head prefect in her school and her mother would not allow her to do housework in case she harmed her hands. We're not told what her older brother Cyril thought about that, but perhaps he didn't do housework either! Mollie went to Teacher Training College for two years, where she sang the principal part of Phyllis in Iolanthe. By 1925 at the opening of Levenshulme High School, Mollie was conducting the choir at a ceremony where The Duchess of Athol was Guest of Honour.

Little Mollie had begun to make her great contribution to the lives of countless young people through teaching and her love of music. In the early years she taught Music and Maths part time at Varna Street boys' school alongside her part time teaching at Levenshulme High School where she eventually became Head of Music. She always claimed that she enjoyed teaching the boys more, because the girls were so giggly. Little Mollie could be big on discipline and was quite forthright in her views about what was right and what was wrong, which didn't go down too well at times with some people, but the youngsters to whom she communicated her love of music knew exactly where they stood. Little Mollie's pursuit of excellence in music loomed large in the memories of many a young person as she encouraged them and sometimes drove them to fulfil their potential.

Testimonies to the impact that Mollie made on many a young life have come from all round the world at Christmas and other times, but it was very special for Mollie last year as she was able to reminisce with some whose lives had been enriched by her contribution at her 90th birthday celebration.

Little Mollie was big on friendship. Her great friend Florence Holgate, who shared her love of music, came to Levenshulme as Head of Maths and later became a live-in lodger with Mollie and her mother. That hospitality was returned after retirement when Florence and Mollie lived for a time with Florence's parents in Accrington. Supportive friendships meant a great deal to Mollie in her later years here in Bramhall. Her brother Cyril who died some years ago had emigrated to New Zealand. Mollie spent some happy holidays in New Zealand and was appreciative of all her distant family's concern for her, but she had no living relatives in this country. The long-standing friendship of Dorothy Broadhurst, Jim & Ada Fairhurst, Charles & Betty Yorke, Robbie and Jen Brunskill and the more recent friendship and practical support given by Mary & Paul Langton and Phyl and Bill Boon provided a substitute local family for Mollie and she made the most of it.

Her friendship with God planted in her early years bore its fruit in the autumn of her life as she was introduced to various activities, many linked with this church. Jen Brunskill recruited Mollie as tea-maker for the recently formed Art group. Ada Fairhurst involved her in the Townswomen's Guild. Accompanying Mary Langton and Phyl Boon to prayer and Bible Study groups was backed up by regular Sunday worship and Mollie coming into membership here on the 15th November 1981.

As her increasing deafness began to isolate her from people, her growth in faith provided for her an inner friendship with God and a tranquillity that was not be disturbed by external circumstances. Little Mollie, in her final years, beset by deafness and the limitations of old age, learned to live in friendship and lean on the best friend of all, Jesus Christ.

I'm told that Mollie, this accomplished pianist, this little woman with a gift for music and a desire to share it with young people, used to conduct the choral music for the Levenshulme High School Speech Day with a clenched fist because she was so short. She always said that she was relieved on those occasions to have her back to the audience and not to have to make a speech. Mollie didn't want centre stage, but the clenched fist says a great deal about her determination and her conducting with back to the audience, but with arms open to those she was leading into a harmonious whole will be a sufficient epitaph for her life.

There's a book that was made into a film entitled, "The Small Woman". It pays tribute to another small woman who was a dedicated missionary, Gladys Aylward. Mollie Buckley follows in a great tradition of people of smaller stature who have sometimes been difficult to cope with, but by their sheer determination have made a real and lasting difference to the lives of others.

We thank God for Mollie and have identified with her suffering by singing earlier:
    O Love that wilt not let me go,
    I rest my weary soul in thee:
    I give thee back the life I owe,
    That in thine ocean depths its flow
    May richer, fuller be.

And now we celebrate her faith and ours by singing:
    Thine be the glory, risen conquering Son,
    Endless is the victory, thou o'er death hast won.

BUTLER: Raymond G. died 24th May 1992 aged 71

Ray Butler was a Civil Servant who worked for the Post Office for more than 40 years. He ended up as a Personnel Manager having worked his way up from being a sorting office clerk and was rewarded, like other long serving Civil Servants with the British Empire Medal. The British Empire Medal is awarded to those who have given long and dedicated service to the Crown. That award symbolises for me, Ray Butler and the kind of person that he became.

RAY WAS A STEADY, RELIABLE SORT OF MAN. Cricket was his first love in sport having played for the church and the Post Office. He loved music, especially the "big band sound" of earlier years, and he sang enthusiastically. How fitting that the last concert he attended in this church was with the Addison Male Voice Choir who epitomised his attitude towards singing. Railways were his hobby, particularly the Great Western Railway, and he did not have to be asked twice to take a trip out to those places where railway enthusiasts meet. Sixteen years ago yesterday, Ray and Mavis married. Her family made him a husband and a grandfather in the same year! Blamed for every card or letter that was late being delivered, he revelled in the good humour that surrounded him. Perhaps the most dramatic change in his life took place when he moved here from his beloved south seven years ago. It can be quite traumatic for someone who has spent a life-time in the south to move north, but Ray loved Bramhall and it showed in a renewed enthusiasm for life.

RAY SERVED THE CROWN, BUT MORE IMPORTANTLY FOR HIM, HE SERVED JESUS CHRIST. He had what St. Paul called the gift of being able "to help others". It didn't matter whether the work needed was in the home, (barring plumbing- there was once a catastrophe there), church or for family or friends, Ray was readily available. He became expert in building castles and drawbridges for fun week, adept in being available to anyone who needed someone to help out in the varied activities of church life. You would expect a Civil Servant to be able to make tea, but Ray was there to do the washing up afterwards. Chairs to be put out, people to be picked up, odd jobs to be done, **Ray was not only willing and able, but he fulfilled the scriptural injunction, "whoever shows kindness to others should do it cheerfully."** Rom:12.8 Ray's commitment to the crown made him the kind of civil servant that he was, but his commitment to Christ made him the kind of person he became. He held office in Cumberland Road Methodist Church, became Treasurer at Pangbourne URC and was soon elected as a Church Meeting representative to the Church Council here in Bramhall. In all his official service to the church there was evidence of his Civil Service background and training. Was there just the hint of the Civil Servant's rule-book mentality in his attitude to community and church life? Were there occasions when Ray had something fixed in his mind and he became what we call stubborn in others and stickability in ourselves? These were the traits that made him ever so human to us. **It was fitting that Ray died on the day when Methodists throughout the world were celebrating John Wesley's experience of the "heart strangely warmed." Wesley has been accused of the same failings!** It was God's love, that fruit of the spirit nurtured in prayer and in his relationship with Jesus Christ that blessed him and us with peace at the end.

THE WORD THAT HAS COME TO MANY PEOPLE'S LIPS IN DESCRIBING RAY IS GENTLE-MAN with the stress on the gentle. Ray Butler was the first person that I visited in Stepping Hill Hospital when I came to Bramhall. From that time to this, in sickness and in health, his life has evidenced a courage and grace that has been an encouragement to me and many others in the church. Our love and prayers, which Ray valued so much, go out now to Mavis his wife, to his daughter Gill and all the family as they cope with their loss. It is not only our love, but God's love and Ray's through the "Communion of Saints" that will reach out to sustain them in the days that lie ahead. Some weeks ago, there was some controversy fuelled by the press because British Empire Medals were not being presented by the Queen to those who had long and loyally served the Crown. Rest assured that Ray by now will have received the only accolade that he ever wanted from His Lord and Master, **"Well done thou good and faithful servant. Come on in and share my happiness."**

BUTTERFIELD: Lily I. died 30th October 1994 aged 79

The question is sometimes asked, "What is a funeral service meant to do?"

First, I believe the funeral service should allow family and friends to "pay their respects" to use a time-honoured phrase. This means that we spend some time reflecting on the life of the person who has died.

Our own memories fill in the gaps as we are reminded of their life and character, have the opportunity of giving thanks to God for their lives and are allowed to come to terms with our natural human sadness.

LILY BUTTERFIELD spent the early part of life in Leeds where she met and married her beloved Arthur. As befits a young couple from that part of Yorkshire their relationship blossomed round a little wooden hut. No not in a park-it was Harry Ramsden's fish and chip shop that was "the night out". Lily was a connoisseur of fish and chips, but none were quite like Harry Ramsden's. You have to wonder whether Harry Ramsden's had a special flavour because Arthur was there too.

Sadly, their time together as a married couple was curtailed by Arthur's time away during the war and he died shortly after returning, leaving Lily to bring up Ann, their five-year-old daughter, on her own.

As might have been expected in those circumstances, Lily's life at that time revolved around doing the best that she could for Ann. A small army pension was supplemented by work as a tailoress and they managed. Everything that Ann achieved was a success for Lily. She was supportive in school life and was there to cheer on Ann as she became a Leeds champion swimmer.

The greatest achievement to come out of that strong relationship was to let go and be positive as Ann met her match in

Brian. The family ties grew stronger as Lily began to enjoy in Brian and the children an extension of her own family life. The move to be near Brian and Ann in Shaw in 1964 and again to this area about seven years ago were only symptomatic of the strength of their family ties.

It would be wrong to give the impression that Lily's life was totally dependent on the family. She was out and about almost every day of her life until recent ill-heath restricted her.

She was an active supporter of the British Legion in younger days and continued in later years to enjoy a full social life. Theatre, bowls, social events at church and frequent use of her pensioner's bus pass made for a very happy retirement with her friends and family. It was those friends and family who were her continuing concern towards the end. When they were happy, she was happy, so we pay our respects

Secondly, the funeral service should allow God to draw near to all those who are present and reassure them of his love for each individual. Sadly, for many of us, it is not until the death of someone that we have known and loved reminds us of our own mortality, that we stop to think serious thoughts about life and death. We are reminded that we cannot shut the door on death. Here we are forced to re-examine our own beliefs about God and how those beliefs about God affect the way in which we live our own lives. We turn our minds to the sovereignty of God who gave life to us and to how Jesus Christ expressed his love for the whole world by dying on the cross.

Grieving is a process that does not begin with death and end with a funeral service. Shock, numbness, fantasies about the future, painful memories and feelings of guilt about the past, affect all of us in different ways according to our relationship with the person who has died.

So, thirdly, a Christian funeral service should bear a public witness to our Christian faith and hope.

The Easter message of the suffering and pain as expressed in our opening hymn, endured by Jesus Christ in his death on the Cross, touches human hearts hurting with the pain of loss.

There is a green hill far away,
Outside a city wall,
Where the dear Lord was crucified,
Who died to save us all.

He died that we might be forgiven,
He died to make us good,
That we might go at last to heaven,
Saved by his precious blood.

The message of his Resurrection restores hope. It's not, "hoping against hope" that the story is true, but a hope borne out of personal experience of the living Lord Jesus Christ. It has been said that Christianity is "caught not taught". If in this funeral service you are helped to reflect upon the life of Lily Butterfield; if here you can experience something of the love of God expressed to you in your loss and can be given renewed hope in life beyond death through the hymns, music, scripture and words shared in this service it will have fulfilled its purpose.

This service will more than fulfil its purpose if just one person present uses this opportunity to renew their own commitment through the church to following Jesus Christ in this life that they may rest assured about the life to come.

For our hope rests in Jesus who said,

"Let not your hearts be troubled, neither let them be afraid"

CHESTER: Alice L. died 2nd March 1997 aged 76

Not many of us who have only known Alice in recent years would associate her with the posh frocks, hats and the Royal Family at Ascot. Those who knew her well would know that her love of the sights and sounds of live racing at Ascot, Uttoxeter or Chester was at one with her love for life itself.

You rarely met Alice without feeling that behind the twinkling eyes there were memories in the mind that seemed to communicate a zest for living no matter what she was involved in. Alice was born in Staffordshire, but lived most of her life in the Stockport area, first over the Heaton's way, but for many years here in Bramhall.

She met her husband-to-be, Donald, in Birmingham during the war. They married in Stockport in 1944 and enjoyed over forty years of life together before Donald died in 1986. They lived in Gawsworth Close from the early days and their only daughter Barbara was brought up in the life of this church. From those early days Alice was associated with the church here, but she only came into membership on the 1/7/1990. Long before that she had become a regular worshipper and active helper in many church activities.

She loved the Pop-In and Tuesday Fellowship. She enjoyed the banter and the practical service given in the work of the Thrift Shop when it was still a cold and draughty cabin. It didn't matter what she was doing from Friday Club to knitting squares for Uganda, Alice was the kind of person who could be counted upon to share in the behind the scenes running of the show.

Alice loved to be involved with people and it showed. I suppose that is why she became an expert on who was doing what to whom in the TV soaps. At home the TV filled her house with people and her generosity of spirit and sense of fun outside made her a good person to share a coffee-making stint with.

Like the rest of us, she could have a moan about those things that upset her, but even the constant pain of arthritis and her knee operation in 1994 did not stop her enjoying life to the full. It was a surprise therefore to all of us when from suspected flu before Christmas there was such a rapid deterioration in health leading to her death just over a week ago.

Alice Chester was above all a thankful person who expressed her gratitude to God and to other people in countless different ways.

She would not forgive me if I did not take this opportunity to say thank you to all of her many friends, especially those of you gathered here today. To the staff of Clumber House, Poynton, for their care over Christmas, and Stepping Hill Hospital for devoted nursing during her final illness. To daughter Barbara, Peter and the family for their constant love and practical help. No sneaky bars of chocolate for you now, Peter.

Above all, I think that Alice would want to say thank you to God. Her simple faith in a God who cared about her and loved her never faltered. It seems a far cry from talking about race meetings and Ascot to talking about Alice and her death.

I'm with Alice in loving the green grass setting of the racecourse with the multi-coloured outfits of jockeys and customers alike with the smell of horses and hot-dog stands. I too enjoy the sound of pounding hooves heard against the background of a crescendo of voices, and the excitement as the horses near the winning post.

I love all of that and believe that heaven will be just as colourful and exciting.

The one thing that I do not like about race meetings is the serious gambling that can cause so much distress to the losers and their families.

People may talk in this life of: "betting your life on there being a God" but you don't have to gamble with God. He sent his only Son to show us exactly what he was like and to prepare the way for us to be with the Father.

Not many people realise that even if you never own a racehorse you can, for a small fee, register your own personal colours with the Jockey Club. The fee for registering personally with God is called faith, and it was Alice's faith in God that gave her the witness to his love in this life and became her passport to the next.

We simply thank God for all that Alice Chester meant to so many people and know that she now enjoys all the colour, the riches and excitement of heaven.

What better hymn to sing on this occasion than?

Guide me, O thou great Jehovah, with its final verse:

When I tread the verge of Jordan,
Bid my anxious fears subside;
Death of death, and hell's destruction,
 Land me safe on Canaan's side:
Songs of praises I will ever give to thee.
Songs of praises I will ever give to thee.

CLARK: Frank M. died 6th January 1996 aged 79

The diminutive comedian Arthur Askey, who died in 1982, used to be described as 'big-hearted' Arthur Askey.

Frank Clark was another little man with a big heart. I think if he were sharing his thoughts about life with you today he would be happy to begin with one of Arthur Askey's catch phrases, **"Hello, playmates."** Life was a lot of fun for Frank and anyone - family, work-colleague or friend, child or adult - became a playmate as they shared different aspects of Frank's life with him.

Frank was born in Misterton, Nottinghamshire, in 1916, of a devoutly Methodist family. His father a Methodist Local Preacher as well as a blacksmith made the gates for the Methodist Church in Misterton. His family background helped lay the foundation for a life-long commitment to Christ and his church that was rooted in faith and worked out in countless practical ways.

Frank was a craftsman by nature as well as by training. Leaving school at 14 he served an engineering apprenticeship at Newall's in Gainsborough for seven years, before moving on to work in the drawing office of Blackburn Aircraft (later to become Hawker Sidley/British Aerospace).

It was a good move for him not only in relation to work, for it brought him close to Hull where Joyce was waiting for her knight in shining armour. His transport was a motor bike rather than a horse but, they met in 1938 at a roller-skating rink, when Frank quite literally fell for Joyce in the process of asking her out.

Two years later in August 1940, Frank and Joyce were married. I love this friend's cartoon of the Nuptial Night with the couple separated by a motor bike and the caption **"Well after all it was my first love."**

The motor bike and Joyce may have been Frank's first love but that affection was soon to be transferred elsewhere. This big-hearted man and some might say even bigger-hearted woman ended up with six children, Heather, Roger, Belinda, Mary, Peter and Beverley.

They, their partners, children and grand-children became the new love of Frank and Joyce's life. The family values shared with Frank and Joyce in their youth and which undergirded their own relationship were communicated by "words, prayers and example"-to use the words of our baptism service - down through the generations. Playmates as well as family they have been in turn to Frank and Joyce, but the fruit of their own relationship of love balanced by discipline, is the example that has continued to be valued by their own family in years gone by.

The immediate family were not the only beneficiaries of Frank's enthusiasm for practical things and his love of life. Friends and neighbours talk appreciatively of Frank's open-hearted love and his willingness to help out wherever help was needed. Frank and Joyce moved here in 1965 when Frank was transferred to Woodford and after a life-time of work in aircraft and related design projects, he finally retired after a period of self-employment at the age of 70.

Retirement simply allowed him more time to indulge his interest in Horology, clock-making for the uninitiated, **Wine & Beer making-like every good Methodist!**-and to take a cookery course along with those other retired refugees from home life Don Mawson and Malcolm Cunningham.

I still think they would have made a very good turn for the Harvest Supper here with their chef's hats on, but it was not to be! Frank Clark, a member of the Church Council and very active Property Steward, will be best remembered here as the Phantom of the Boiler House emerging from depths after dealing with the vagaries of the church heating system.

I think that even Frank, with all his dogged perseverance was ready to admit defeat as keeper of the keys of the church. Despite his best efforts, maintenance of security with 80 plus front door keys proved to be an impossible task. **Nevertheless, his unfailing good humour made playmates of us all** as he tried to locate a key that had been transferred on without reference to him or when one of us would try to argue the case for an additional key to be issued for our own particular needs.

That good humour was maintained in the face of growing health problems and the increased concern of family and friends alike. When I saw Frank at home just before Christmas he was a little weary of the constant health problems, but as confident as ever in the love that came down at Christmas.

A friend writing a card of sympathy quotes for the clock man, **"The clock of life is wound but once and no man has the power to tell just when the hands will stop at late or early hour."** The hands of the clock of life may have stopped suddenly for Frank, but his faith lives on in the lives of those whom he has touched.

As Big-hearted Frank says good-bye to his playmates, I think that he might use another of Arthur Askey's catch phrases in closing, **"Ay thang yew!" "Ay thang yew!"**

Because above all Frank was a thankful man, thankful for Joyce and the family, thankful for friends and his church family, thankful to God who blessed him and blessed others through him.

We thank God for him.

COASE: Win died 2nd February 1995 aged 77

Win Coase was in the process of moving from her home of twenty odd years in Perth Close to a flat in Damery Court when she became seriously ill and was taken into Ormskirk District General Hospital. Within a matter of days, we were saddened to learn of her death. I suppose most of us who knew of the impending move reflected on the timing of her death and my sharing today is prompted by thoughts of Win's move from the place she called home.

Like most of us, Win had called several places home in her life. Born in North Manchester in 1918 when people in Europe were anticipating the peace and prosperity that would flow from the bloody sacrifice of the Great War. Studdert-Kennedy, better known as Woodbine Willie, was expressing the ordinary soldier's hopes of a better home in Old England.

> "What I says is, sink old England,
> To the bottom of the sea!
> It's new England as I fights for,
> It's an England swep' aht clean,
> It's an England where we'll get at
> Things our eyes 'ave never seen;
> Decent wages, justice mercy,
> And a chance for ev'ry man,
> For to make 'is 'ome an 'eaven,
> If 'e does the best 'e can."

Home is where hopes can be realised, but Win like so many of you lived through the disillusionment that set in during the twenties with their strikes and the great depression of the thirties culminating in yet another war that would devastate Europe yet again.

Win's experience of those years of economic deprivation for so many gave her an abiding concern for less fortunate people in this land which she was proud to call her home.

Win Coase, with her husband George, lived and worked in different places during those years. The war years found George working with the fire service in Liverpool, Win with Vickers at Trafford Park and living together in the family home at Crumpsall. The close family ties cemented then meant that even after the death of her husband in 1970 and the subsequent move to Bramhall, Win continued to keep the home together for her teen-age son and care for aging parents.

Win worked for a few years after her move to Bramhall, but slowly as her family circumstances changed, she was able to enjoy again many of the pleasures of younger days. Ballet and ice skating were her great loves.

Ice dancing with George at Cheetham Hill Ice Rink was not quite the same as the glamour and grace of a performance by Torvill and Dean, but how appropriate that Win's last real night out should be at their show on the 7th January this year. That night of enjoyment summed up the loving relationship that she has shared with her family, especially Robert, Alison, Joanne, Stephen.

Win's garden was an extension of her home and the weeds found there were attacked just as vigorously as the dust in the living room. Win was a perfectionist; she couldn't abide sloppiness. Always immaculate herself, she made sure that those things for which she was responsible were done well.

The lovely thing was that Win was also an appreciative person.

"Bramhall in Bloom" gave her the opportunity not only of enjoying other people's gardens, but also sharing her appreciation of beautiful things with those who went with her, as well as those who opened up their gardens to visitors.

Win's third home was her church. Early days associated with the Anglican Church at St. Mary's, Higher Crumpsall, brought a commitment that continued here in Bramhall as this church became her spiritual home.

Win was not an up-front kind of leader, but she was totally involved in anything to which she belonged whether that was the Townswomen's Guild or a Fellowship Group in the church. Hymns were not simply sung in church or fellowship group, but the words were prayed through at home. The faithfulness that made her an ever-present at worship on Sundays meant that you could count on her to do those things which were part of her commitment to Jesus Christ and His church.

Win Coase has now gone to her final home with God her Father. She will love it there because anywhere that God is present is a place of justice, love, grace, and beauty. I want to close by reading a passage from the New Testament that seems to sum up the relationship between our home on earth and that which we find in heaven.

Read 2 Cor 5 v 1-10 "For we know that if the earthly tent we live in is destroyed, we have a building from God, a house not made with hands, eternal in the heavens……….."

That's where Win is now!

COOKE: George died 8th May 1995 aged 85

Have you ever come to the end of a very long day worn out? Physically, mentally, emotionally, yes even spiritually, you are tired out and you know that if you sit down, you will never make it up the stairs to bed. You head for your bed, collapse into it and drop off into a deep and dreamless sleep. George Cooke had come to the end of a very long, 85 years long in fact, and tiring day. He was physically, mentally and spiritually exhausted when he dropped off into his final sleep. In his day George had enjoyed living a very full life and he had certainly lived life to the full.

George became a Fellow of the Institute of Mechanical Engineers the hard way, by attending night school and taking exams alongside gaining good, practical experience in the field. His working life first with ICI and then with Simon Carves Ltd designing boilers for Power Stations took him all over the world. In Germany he found a second home, learning to speak the language fluently and becoming a connoisseur of their wines. George was a well-read man with an enquiring mind who never stopped learning and was full of questions about life even to the end.

His scientific turn of mind spilled over into his enthusiasm for photography which was not always shared by the family. Prize-winning photography is rarely enhanced by a pose that has at least one member of the family sticking out their tongue at the photographer. George shared with his growing family his own life-long love for the arts with visits to concerts, the theatre and ballet. The sensitivity to others that was always there in him balanced his own enthusiasm for cultural visits to historical places like Stratford upon Avon, with a week at the seaside for the family. As the family of three, Marjorie, Geoffrey and John grew through marriage to include four grand-children and two great-grandchildren so did George and his late-wife Louise's capacity for hospitality at Christmas and birthdays. Mind you, it was never quite clear whether these family meals were provided for others or for George to show how much he enjoyed his food.

Retirement for George was hardly that, as he took on more and more responsibilities with voluntary work that earned him the UMIST Medal and a social life that had him involved in everything from Probus to the Walkers club. George would want to say thank you to those who encouraged, supported and latterly helped him to live life to the full. Also for the practical, but not claustrophobic care of a loving family, with John & Ann, living locally, bearing the brunt of the day-to-day concern. For the caring friends and neighbours from outside as well as within the church. The death of George's partner of 56 years, Louise, on the 28/4/92 saw him with the encouragement of neighbours, Sandy and Margaret Simpson, who unfortunately cannot be here today, returning to his spiritual roots in the Methodist Church. Early days as a Sunday School teacher and even pursuing Louise by joining the church choir, to which she already belonged, had laid the foundation of a faith in God and a relationship with Jesus Christ which George never really lost.

Links with the church, which had become tenuous, were reinforced in regular worship and as a tearaway George on his motorised wheelchair terrorised the pavements and made every opportunity to share in the coffee and social activities of the church. The ready smile and the willingness to spend time in conversation never left George. Many people were encouraged as this man in the motorised wheelchair made the most of the rest of his life. On my bookshelves I have a book in which a number of well-known people share briefly their thoughts about death. Its title says quite simply, "Bid the World Good-night". George Cooke, after a very full and well-lived day, has quite simply "Bid the World Good-night". He knew for himself, and would want you to remember, the words of the Apostle Paul who said,

"Our brothers, we want you to know the truth about those who have died, so that you will not be sad, as those who have no hope. We believe that Jesus died and rose again, and so we believe that God will take back with Jesus those who have died believing in him." 1 Thess. 4.13

That certainly applies to George Cooke!

CORRIE: Ellen (Nellie) died 31st May 1993 aged 100

Some years ago, when I was visiting Northern Ireland, I was told about a Lord Mayor who went to see a 100-year-old lady and began his conversation with a question, "Have you lived here all your life?" to which the 100-year-old responded, "Not yet, not yet." No, the 100-year-old was not Nellie Corrie, but it might have been. It's that kind of confidence, determination, yes, even stubbornness, that characterised the life of Nellie Corrie. Even when I came here about six years ago there was talk already of Nellie being the kind of person who would hang on until she was a hundred. Every time I saw her, she would remind me proudly, "I'm your oldest member."

BORN ON THE 10th JANUARY 1893 in Wilmslow, and what a picture that conjures up of a long-gone Victorian age, Nellie was the youngest child in a family of seven who survived infancy. With five of the others being boys, and little but the flickering of a more modern attitude to the role of women, it can be imagined who shared most of the burden with her mother for the domestic work needed in the home. At the age of three Nellie moved to the village of Bramhall where educational opportunities were limited by family resources and the attitudes prevalent at that time. Nevertheless, Nellie made the most of the village elementary school in Bramhall and her own reading and writing of historical essays and poetry developed an already lively mind. It was this mind that even in her 90's, loved to tell of the beginnings of Bramhall's development from a village into a small town.

THE CORRIE FAMILY PLAYED THEIR OWN PART in that development. Her father established two businesses in Bramhall, each of which contributed in its own way from Victorian days to the beginning of the 1960's to that development. It was Nellie's responsibility to keep the books of the business for many years. The family as a whole and Nellie's father in particular were part of the team that built the chapel here in which we now worship.

This building was officially opened on May 4th 1905 and the Corrie family have been associated with the growth of the Methodist Church here from that time to this. Nellie's first love here in younger days was teaching in the Sunday School, but she was drawn into countless other activities both inside and outside the church.

Strange isn't it that she ended her days in Hillbrook, where she has been for the past 17 years, the home where she attended training classes for young Sunday School teachers more than 80 years ago.

NELLIE WAS AT HOME IN HILLBROOK in more ways than one.

At home with her surroundings which had their own memories for her;

at home with the long-time friends that she found there;

at home with the love and care lavished upon her by the staff at Hillbrook and the friends that visited.

In these later years, for perhaps the first time in her life, she became the focus of everyone's love and attention.

She enjoyed it and mellowed.

THEY SAY THAT WHAT WE ARE AT 9 WE SHALL BE AT 90.

I suppose that might be illustrated in the determination displayed in Nellie's survival, both in those early and these later years. But as with most sayings it does not tell the whole truth.

For as long as anyone can remember there lay on Nellie's bedside table a Bible, latterly a large print edition of the NIV New Testament and Psalms, and her precious prayer book, the Methodist Hymn Book, that had belonged to her elder sister Margaret. From 1962 onwards it was used, almost to destruction.

There was also a book called, "The Voice of Prayer" and a book given her earlier in 1936 by Miss Florence Rowbotham, a great stalwart of this church. This was worn out by the 1980's and had to be replaced by the family. I don't think that Nellie would be upset with the title of that book as her epitaph. It is called "Being and Doing".

"BEING AND DOING", a selection of Helpful Thoughts for daily reading was Nellie's personal guide to Christian living for over 50 years.

The Bible, the Methodist Hymn Book, the Voice of Prayer and Being and Doing combined to change the rather austere and sometimes off-putting woman of younger days into a more faith-full, grace-full and thankful lady in these latter years.

The book "Being and Doing" has it in the right order.

Being in Jesus Christ in this life, Nellie began to do what Jesus Christ wanted her to do.

Doing what Jesus wanted her to do, she became more like the kind of person Jesus wanted her to be.

No, she wasn't the same person at ninety as she was at nine.

JESUS MADE HER DIFFERENT.
SHE'S DIFFERENT AGAIN NOW,
BUT STILL "IN CHRIST JESUS".

CORRIE: Freda died 4th February 1993 aged 69

Freda Corrie was one of the fastest things on two legs ever seen around the village of Bramhall. Even when she was using her stick in later years you almost had to jog to keep up with her. There was an urgency about her walking that gives a clue about her character.

FREDA IS PART OF THE HISTORY OF BRAMHALL VILLAGE AND OF THE FOLK-LORE OF THIS METHODIST CHURCH.

Her inner urgency allowed her time to be involved in so many things that lesser mortals can only marvel at. Freda was never content simply to belong to an organisation, she actively contributed to its growth and well-being. The Women's Institute and the Women's Royal Voluntary Service might claim her as their own, but there can be no doubt where Freda's first love was. It was with young people.

It might have been expected that she would meet her husband Kenneth leaping around the church badminton court. Her enthusiastic participation in such activities continued in a lifetime's service to young people of all ages.

Freda was the youth club of this church for more years than most people can remember. She had the gift of remaining youthful in style, approach and even dress as the ages rolled by.

It was Freda, the Leader of the youth club, who was ever available to take the youngsters away to the extra activities like the Methodist Association of Youth Clubs' London Weekend.

It was Freda the Christian leader, who made it easier for many young people to find faith in Jesus Christ.

THE VERY YOUNG HAD A VERY SPECIAL PLACE IN FREDA'S HEART.

Down the years she not only ran the Beginners' class of the Sunday School here, she herself became the Beginners' class. Tributes have poured in from those whose lives she touched in Sunday School as she introduced them to the love of God. In younger days she bounced about with the best of them in action choruses and dramatically led story-telling. Self-prepared visual aids were her forte long before "visual aids" were the "in" thing or her son Andrew joined the B.B.C. Her Sunday School training classes became a breeding ground for new teachers who would put into practice what they learned from Freda in the various departments of the Sunday School.

THE URGENCY THAT CHARACTERISED FREDA'S LIFE SOMETIMES MADE HER SEEM A LITTLE ABRUPT TO THOSE WHO DIDN'T KNOW HER SO WELL.

She would listen to what others were saying but, when she had made up her mind about anything, she had her head down and she was off. Woe betides anyone who happened to stand in the way. The urgency that was so much part of her travelling between ideas and places hardly showed at all when she had arrived. She became patience personified in dealing with the problems of the young, in caring for her husband Kenneth for many years before his death just over twelve months ago, and in visiting Hillbrook Grange to see Aunt Nellie Corrie who was a hundred on the 10th of last month. Sadly, Freda who had visited so faithfully could not be there for that special occasion.

FREDA'S FINAL ILLHESS WAS THANKFULLY BRIEF.

She felt unwell after attending the King's College carol service just before Christmas and a few weeks later we mourn her death. The urgency that was so much a part of her being was lived out to the death.

She was ready for the next stage of her life and would have been able to identify with the Apostle Paul when he said, "I want very much to be with Christ, which is a far better thing." Freda had not spent a lifetime teaching the Christian faith without experiencing what it meant to be "In Christ" in this life. Her own experience of Jesus Christ was what determined the urgency with which she sought to share His love.

AT THE VERY CENTRE OF THE CORRIE FAMILY'S LIFE WAS THE LOVE OF GOD.

"As a family" Freda was able to say, "we have so much love for each other that there is plenty to spare for other people." It is God's love shared through Freda down the years that prompted the flood of letters and cards that so surprised her in hospital and again has encouraged Andrew during the past few days.

It was God's love that Freda continued to share in encouraging her non-church-going companions in hospital to join her in going to worship in the hospital chapel at Wythenshawe.

It was God's love seen in Freda that motivated those who so willingly shared in a rota of caring for her at Andrew's home. Freda enjoyed God's love in life and continues to abide in it in death. Come to think of it, 'abiding' is something you can't imagine Freda doing. Perhaps she will team up with her old friends Peter Roberts and Stan Nicol to run a youth club in heaven.

A church friend sent me a calendar quote for Saturday 6th Feb which seemed so appropriate for this occasion.

"They that sow in tears shall reap in joy." Ps.125.6

That's our prayer and a promise for Andrew and the family.

CORRIE: Kenneth P. died 12th December 1991 aged 77

Kenneth Corrie was baptised in this church and has had a lifetime's association with it. To read out the list of the responsibilities that he undertook is to go through a what's what of Church life. Junior Church member, Teacher, Pianist, and until 5 years ago Treasurer. Youth Leader, Member of the Choir for 50 years and the organist. Poor Steward, Door Steward, Chapel Steward and on the Property Committee. He was a Trustee, a member of the Leaders Meeting long before Church Councils were invented, and involved at Circuit and District level. Here we have a man who was so involved in every aspect of church life that he was well qualified to reflect on the organisation of the church, warts and all.

Even a saint could not have been so directly involved at the centre of church life without bearing some scars and Kenneth Corrie would be the first to admit that he was no saint. Kenneth had strong views and could give and take with the best of them, but he always had the interests of the church at heart. His background as part of the Corrie family historically associated with Bramhall village gave him a different perspective to those who moved into the rapidly growing village, but no one could fault his love for both the village and this church. Kenneth, as an organist, was better placed than most to reflect on what was important in funeral services. The choice of hymns this morning is an expression of his feeling that those who conduct funeral services should make sure that we "LET THE PEOPLE LEAVE WITH HOPE." For a few minutes now I want to share with you something of the hope that Kenneth Corrie was talking about. Kenneth's faith was in the "Almighty power of God" which he saw expressed in the power and beauty found in Creation. Despite many years of ill-health, he was able to hold on to a faith in the ultimate power and goodness of God.

One of the verses that is missing from "I sing the almighty power of God" in our current hymn books would best explain Kenneth's faith.

Creatures (as numerous as they be) Are subject to thy care;
There's not a place where we can flee But God is present there.

Kenneth Corrie knew that presence in a more personal way, through the coming of Jesus Christ. No-one who knew Kenneth would put him in the category of what is termed evangelical Christians who talk a great deal about personal faith. What was clear to anyone who talked with him was that there was at the root of his practical Christianity a faith in Christ that watered the roots to produce the fruit.

It is sometimes difficult for those who have always belonged to the church to point to a time when they became more than church-goers. Kenneth knew, despite the doubts and fears that come to us all, that he not only belonged to the church, but that he also belonged to Jesus Christ. That was the hope that sustained him and is the hope in which he would want you to leave this service.

We have talked about faith; we have talked about hope. What about love? Love was something that Kenneth knew a lot about. Together Kenneth and Freda have shared a love that has sustained them both in their faith and hope. In recent years Kenneth has been on the receiving end of a great deal of sacrificial love expressed through Freda's caring. That love shown by Freda and Andrew helped Kenneth to hold on through the suffering of these last years, but even that love is but a pale reflection of the love that God has for each one of us. To do what Kenneth asked, "TO LET YOU LEAVE IN HOPE" I can point only to the power of the God foundational to his faith: the coming of Jesus that brings us hope; and the presence of the Holy Spirit that shares with us God's love and prompts us to share it with one another. Kenneth's hope is now fulfilled in Christ. Hear the message in his chosen hymn:

> **Joy to the world, The Lord is come!**
> **Let earth receive her King;**
> **Let every heart prepare him room,**
> **And heaven and nature sing. (x 3)**

DAVENPORT: Bryan M. died 18th March 1994 aged 52

In 1962 the Queen sent out just 393 100th birthday telegrams. Last year she sent 100th birthday congratulations to 2,869 men and women. Obviously, when a man like Bryan dies aged 52 in these days many of us question why. Bryan was dedicated to God through baptism in this church and was brought up in a loving Christian home. Christian parents, Arthur & Nellie, the Sunday School and the church were the strong influences upon his childhood years. After moving about the country with his father's work, the family with his two sisters, Jean and Rosemary settled back in this area and Bryan completed his education at King's School, Macclesfield. He joined Thomas Cook the travel agents and worked there until taking early retirement last year. He met his wife to be, Val at Thomas Cook's and they shared many happy years as the marriage was blessed with Stuart in 1967, and Diana in 1970. Parental pride was fulfilled. Val and Bryan were present as Stuart was awarded his B.A.(Hons) degree and also when Diana married Ric in 1991. Bryan admitted on that occasion that he wasn't losing a daughter, but gaining a mechanic. A mechanic was all he needed in the family because he himself was a very practical man. Gardening, do-it-yourself and above all cooking everything from curries to Christmas cake won him the plaudits of the family if not prizes in competitions. In December last year Bryan was able to make good use of all his skills as he shared in the running of the Plough Boy Inn at Disley. This was the Bryan Davenport that most of you knew. A man who loved life, his family, his work and his friends. **The other Bryan would be able to identify with the author of the next hymn chosen by the family.** William Cowper, one of the leading English poets suffered from depression for much of his life. All of his hymns are worth reading by anyone who struggles to understand the goodness of God in a wayward world.

None is better than this hymn, number 65 in our hymn book, **"GOD MOVES IN A MYSTERIOUS WAY HIS WONDERS TO PERFORM."**
This is, without doubt, the greatest hymn ever written on the mystery of God's working in the world which he created.

Two themes are interwoven in the hymn. Our bewilderment in the face of inexplicable happenings in the world and our confidence in a God who continues to be in control.

THE BEGINNING OF THE HYMN reminds us that God's ways are not our ways. His ways are mysterious, but there at the very centre of the confusion God is moving his wonders to perform.

AS THE POET PROCEEDS, he tells us that we are not at the mercy of a divine roulette wheel of chance, but part of God's bright design. I still find it helpful to think of what we see of things that disturb us in the world as like looking at the stitching side of a tapestry, all wiggly threads of different colours with lots of loose ends. It's only God who sees the final design which is the beautiful side of that same tapestry. "Ye fearful saints, fresh courage take," You'll need that courage, but it is courage backed by faith in a God who cares for you and the whole world. You cannot see the sunshine when it is hidden by the clouds, but the pilot who flies the Thomas Cook's tours will tell you that it is always there above the clouds. "Behind a frowning providence He hides a smiling face." "The bud may have a bitter taste, but sweet will be the flower."

FINALLY, We are encouraged not to try and make sense of it by reason alone, "Judge not the Lord by feeble sense, but trust him for his grace." It's our belief in the grace and goodness of God as shown to us in Jesus Christ that allows us to walk the tightrope between a kind of false piety that seems to suggest that suffering and the death of a loved one does not hurt and the "blind unbelief" that destroys all faith in anything beyond death. Bryan knew, like William Cowper, what it felt like to be stressed and depressed. People can be brought through such experiences by the love of friends, the love of family and the love of God, but not without cost. "Love hurts" is more than the title of a T.V. series. God experienced that as His only Son became part of the mystery of suffering and death on a cross. Love is victorious when even death cannot destroy it. Love never ends!

Sadness and suffering are part of the cost of loving.
Eternal life, lived in love is the reward of faith in Jesus Christ.

DENNIS: Daniel H. died 26th March 1994 aged 91

I was talking to someone about Dan Dennis earlier this week and he said to me, **"Dan Dennis was a big man in every way."** Physically he was certainly that, a great big bear of a man, but despite his size his demeanour gave much more the impression of a cuddly Koala bear rather than a great growling grizzly. There was a gentleness about Dan Dennis that was inherent in his nature, but all of that is to jump ahead of his story. Much is made of family environment in these days, but Dan didn't have an easy time of it. Born 14th Sept 1902, he was the second of four boys brought up by his grandmother when his mother died. He was just 16 at the time, but was fortunate to become an apprentice engineer at Chatham dockyard. The discipline and skills learned in that apprenticeship were to stand him in good stead for a lifetime's career providing the civilian engineering support for our navy and its dockyards.

This basically shy young man, trained in Chatham dockyard, travelled widely and gained much experience of life in the Mediterranean and near east with the Royal Fleet Auxiliary. That experience and even life working at the Admiralty in London didn't make it any easier for him to handle his feelings for the attractive young Win who had lived in the same street in Gillingham. Dan was the ripe old age of thirty-three before he got round to marrying Win, but they wasted no time then in producing Anne and David, and settling down to family life. It suited Dan, the sporting young man, who turned his hands to most things including gardening, jam-making and stuffing turkeys for Christmas. Despite spending four years during the war without the family on the besieged island of Malta, Dan and Win's love gave their family life a stability and security that has had its effect down the generations. The rattling of the milk bottles was sufficient to keep discipline and indicate Dad's displeasure at late night doorstepping by Anne and David. Anne's husband Stan Nicol, who died less than two years ago was blessed by this family haven of love and peace. Their children Alison, Sheena and Ian have treasured it and found in it a model for their own behaviour and married life.

This patriarchal figure of Dan was a Bird's Eye captain without the beard as he told the tales of his youth and his adventures in Malta. David and Elizabeth's children, Kristina, Catherine and Andrew, brought up in Canada and with more infrequent contact with Dan and Win, write movingly and lovingly of their influence upon their lives and standards. How does the hymn go? "Scenes by the wayside, tales of the sea, Stories of Jesus tell them to me."

In some way, every story Dan told about himself was a story also about his own maturing relationship with Jesus Christ. Jesus was the inspiration for Dan's life from his earliest days in Christmas Street Church in Gillingham, Kent. Lovely name for a church, with reminders of the birth of Jesus. Certainly, Jesus was born in Dan's heart in those early days and all of his service in and through the church became a natural progression from that time. Band of Hope, singing in the choir, and making his home in different churches as he travelled. Society Steward and Sunday School superintendent in Rosyth where the family moved just before the war, and later here in Bramhall. Similar responsibilities as a leader in the church followed in Bramhall after Dan and Win moved here in 1955.

After retirement, Tuesday Fellowship, Probus and Art Group came to the fore, but his first love in church life was always Local Preaching. He qualified as a Local Preacher in 1948 and it was a great pleasure for all of us here in the presence of his family to acknowledge his 40 years of preaching as he spoke on Christmas Day 1988 on, "A Christmas I have known". Mind you, from church life I like best the story of the minister at Rosyth, a little man Mr. Foxon, meeting Dan for the first time after the war and taking a chair to stand on so that he could shake his hand. A big man indeed, in every way, of stature, in family and church life. A big man but a quiet, gentle man. A gentleman of his age nurtured in the early part of this century and unwilling to be pushed into the desperate urgency demanded by those who live their lives in the fast lane of the second half of the 20th century. **"We live more simply, that others may simply live."**, was more than a Christian Aid slogan to Dan.

He never owned a car and his bike in the garage is a vintage model that must be worth a bob or two. Win might have thought at times that certain matters deserved more urgent attention than Dan was prepared to give them but as the children say-they never saw Dan get upset, "Even when Nana was going on about things!" **"Be calm"** he would say to others, and he was, even to the last evening of his life. I joined Win and Anne singing hymns being chosen by Dan at his hospital bedside and later he calmly and clearly talked about how his books might be passed on to other Local Preachers.

We prayed together just after 10 o'clock and he died as peacefully as he had lived, just after midnight.

That's why I think it is so appropriate that today's funeral service should be on Maundy Thursday. It's today that the church commemorates the time when Jesus demonstrated his way of living by washing the disciples' feet before sharing with his closest disciples in that communion of the Last Supper. Dan lived in the way demonstrated by Jesus and he died in close communion with Christ. He would want you now to share in that close communion as you hear Dan's words on the lips of Jesus from that "Upper Room" saying to you, **"Be calm, be calm."**

Try this adaptation of the words of Jesus and read the words of the Gospel hymns chosen for this service if you are in any way troubled by Dan Dennis' death or that of a loved one on this Maundy Thursday.

"Calm I leave with you; my calm I give to you; not as the world gives do I give to you. Let not your hearts be troubled, neither let them be afraid."

HYMN 689 Will your anchor hold in the storms of life
HYMN 180 When I survey the wondrous cross
HYMN 212 Thine be the glory, risen conquering Son,
          Endless is the victory, thou o'er death hast won.

EDWARDS: F. Margaret died 31ˢᵗ March 1994 aged 85

The question is sometimes asked, "What is a funeral service meant to do?" **First, I believe the funeral service should allow family and friends to "pay their respects".** This means that we spend some time reflecting on the life of the person who has died. Our own memories fill in the gaps as we are reminded of their life and character. We have the opportunity of giving thanks to God for their lives; and are allowed to come to terms with our natural human sadness. Margaret was brought up and educated in the lovely city of Chester. She moved to Stretford in the twenties and found employment as a secretary with what was then Metropolitan Vickers. She must have done well there. She went on to become private secretary to the Head of the Research Department, Sir Arthur Fleming, who was also a Director at Manchester United. Margaret married her late husband, Frank, just after the war. **As the custom was, she gave up her own career for that of a homemaker for Frank in Hale and was later mother to Sue.** The family was always important to Margaret and her own three times a Sunday at church as a youngster ensured a Christian background for Sue. Margaret kept in touch with the extended Edwards family and she was noted for remembering everyone's birthdays and special occasions. Her later years in Bramhall were enriched by two very different grandchildren in Donna and Therese. She loved and cared for them both. Margaret enjoyed music, gardening and holidays in Scotland and with her sister, who died last year in Portishead, near Bristol. She found the onset of old age difficult to cope with and especially after the stroke, hated the thought of being dependent upon others. She appreciated the loving care of family and medical staff alike, but like most active people made a poor patient. She was not afraid of death and it came at the right time peacefully in old age as a welcome friend. For that we thank God.

Secondly, the funeral service should allow God to draw near to all those who are present and reassure them of His love for each individual. Sadly, for many of us, it is not until the death of someone that we have known and loved reminds us of our own mortality that we stop to think serious thoughts about life and death. We are reminded that we cannot shut the door on death. Here we are forced to re-examine our own beliefs about God and how those beliefs about God affect the way in which we live our own lives. **We turn our minds to the sovereignty of God who gave life and in Jesus Christ expressed his love for the whole world.** Grieving is a process that does not begin with death and end with a funeral service. Shock, numbness, fantasies about the future, painful memories and feelings of guilt about the past affect all of us in different ways according to our relationship with the person who has died. The process of grieving with its sadness and tears is helped when the harsh reality of death is softened by what someone once described to me as, "being wrapped in the warm blanket of God's love". That leads us on to the third function of a funeral service.

Thirdly, a Christian funeral service should bear a public witness to our Christian faith and hope. The Easter message of the suffering and pain endured by Jesus Christ in his death on the Cross touches human hearts hurting with the pain of loss; the message of his Resurrection restores hope. It's not "hoping against hope" that the story is true, but a hope borne out of personal experience of the living Lord Jesus Christ. It has been said that Christianity is, "caught not taught". **If in this funeral service you are helped to catch something from your memories of Margaret that gives you faith in a living and loving Lord,** if you can experience something of the love of God expressed to you in your loss and can be given renewed hope in life beyond death through the hymns, music, scripture and words shared in this service it will have fulfilled its purpose. The service will more than fulfil its purpose if just one person present uses this opportunity to renew their own commitment to following Jesus Christ in this life that they may rest assured about the life to come. For our hope rests on Jesus who said, "Let not your hearts be troubled, believe in God, believe also in me."

**So, we sing, "Lord of all hopefulness, Lord of all joy,
Whose trust, ever childlike, no cares could destroy.**

EVERARD: Hilda died 4th April 1994 aged 85

A few days after Hilda Everard was born, Henry Ford redeemed his promise to produce, "a motor car for the great multitude". Hilda Everard was one of that great multitude of ordinary people, but I'm not aware that she ever owned a Model T Ford in its only colour, black. Incidentally, if you want a black car now, it has to be ordered specially and costs more. They call that progress!!

Real progress was something few people knew much about in the years immediately before and after the First World War. Ordinary people like Hilda were fortunate if they managed a reasonable education and found a job that brought in a little money. The machinist in a clothing factory married the railway engineer, Norman, just before the Second World War, and the couple moved from Nottingham to live and work in Doncaster for most of the war years.

The birth of baby David in 1939 didn't quite cause this country to go to war, which is rather surprising because he has given us problems ever since. Mind, you couldn't say that to Hilda, because she doted on David and in the way of mothers of that bygone age waited on him hand and foot. What a shock to David's system when he went away for three years National Service and tried singing, "Kiss me good-night Sergeant Major".

Some of the younger generation find it difficult to understand why the older ones amongst us look back to those earlier years and always picture them in black and white. Real community life in those days in places like Nottingham, to which they returned in 1944, was made up of streets and backalleys with middens.

Neighbours formed their own social and community care clubs, looking after each other when emergencies beset family life. Friends did everything from looking after each other's children to laying out the bodies of their loved ones at death.

You can imagine the response, to the Trent bursting its banks in 1947 and picture the local newspapers' photograph of the boat sailing down the Everard's street to hand bread buns to those trapped in the upstairs bedrooms.

Our memories are in black and white because that was how the world seemed in those gloomy post-war years.

No wonder Hilda, like so many others, relieved the gloom by visits to the cinema with her friend. Tuesday and Friday, regular as clockwork, until the mid-fifties and the onset of television. The foundations had been laid for television to become Hilda's great companion in her later years after the death of her husband Norman in 1976.

I suppose most people would have thought of Hilda as one of the multitude in terms of church affiliation. In her early days she was nurtured in the Wilfred Road Methodist church, Nottingham, but most of her life was spent as part of the worshipping fellowship at Bridgeway Hall Methodist Church.

Hilda was not one for the limelight, but she worshipped regularly and used her gifts, including that of pianist, wherever they were needed, in the choir and in the life and work of the various organisations within the church.

That's the trouble with the multitude of ordinary church members, you hardly notice they are there until they have gone. There was never any question about Hilda being there until old age and ill health began to overtake her.

It was lovely to see her making the effort to be part of worship here when she moved up to Disley Grange last October and she did appreciate all the love and concern that was shared with her for such a brief time.

Have you ever wondered what happened to the multitudes that Jesus spoke to in his ministry on earth? Some of them, I am sure, responded to his message. They weren't of the twelve, or even the seventy who were sent out, but they were the unseen and unheralded witnesses who prepared the way for the rapid growth of the early church.

Hilda was one of that multitude who lived and died in the peace that she found in the Lord Jesus Christ. She may never have become one of the multitude for whom Henry Ford produced his model T Ford, but there is no doubt that she was one of the multitude for whom Christ died. That gives us the assurance that she now lives with Him.

The hymns chosen for this service:

"In heavenly love abiding" and
"Great is thy faithfulness" sum up the faith of Hilda Everard.

Perhaps the music and words of:

"Make me a channel of your peace"

can be used as a challenge for us too.

FEARNS: Hilda F. died 16th May 1988 aged 81

With permission, I want to preface my words with something said by someone talking to Joan a few days ago about Hilda. "We all love her, you know" that person said, **"We all love her, you know."** That's reassuring isn't it for all who loved her referred to friends who knew her well. Many people have spoken to me of Hilda's indomitable spirit as she fought back from an earlier illness. A lady who had the courage to go through the difficult times and come up smiling. As so often that single-minded determination can be difficult to live with.

Hilda knew her own mind and was prepared to express it forcefully where necessary. A few weeks ago, I talked in a sermon about many a northerner "who was prepared to call a spade a spade, who never got round to digging with it." Hilda's single-mindedness was redeemed by a willingness to care in practical ways. She was still visiting "the old ones" as she put it when she herself was definitely in that category!

"We all love her", was said from the hearts of people who were not blind to her faults, but recognised the authentic stamp of caring love in her service to others. The kind of caring and concern that continued even after she collapsed and was taken into hospital.

All who loved her included her family, daughters Joan and Ann and their families. My son likes to remind us that two negatives make a positive, which is why he is so wonderful really! All of us have within us, for good or for ill, that which is inherited from our family, something of our parents' identity. All of us have that background and training that continues with us as a result of our home environment and upbringing. None of us would pretend that everything that happens within the four walls of any home is always harmony and light, but the home lubricated by love, becomes a place within which each one of us can grow.

We like to talk of mellowing with age in human terms, but isn't there also in the lives of older Christians something of the fruit of the Spirit: love, joy, peace, patience, kindness, goodness, etc. ?The Fearns family clearly loved a mother and a grandmother who loved them. All who loved Hilda, I'm sure, included God. I'm not sure that Hilda ever took up a leading role in the life of the church. In all her many years she was not one of the performers, so well-remembered in the church. Hilda simply belonged.

Hilda belonged:

in a way that influenced her family and was clear to her friends;

as she sat on our settee at one of our birthday gatherings, cheerfully joining in the fun and games that are part and parcel of these events;

in a way that endeared her to passing acquaintances as well as church friends in worship and at the Tuesday Fellowship.

Hilda belonged to a God who loved her, as we do too. As I was rounding off what to say this morning our Quite Time prayers shared this passage from Jeremiah 32: 38-41:

"They will be my people and I will be their God. I will give them singleness of heart and action so that they will always fear me for their own good and the good of their children after them. I will make an everlasting covenant with them. I will never stop doing good to them, and I will inspire them to fear me, so that they will never turn away from me. I will rejoice in doing them good and will assuredly plant them in the land with all my heart and soul."

Hilda Fearns, a lady loved, after God's own heart, who believed and belonged in this life is surely with her friend and her God in the life to come.

FLINT: Cyril died 11th August 1996 aged 63

Someone said to me recently, "Every time that I go to a funeral service, I learn something about the person who has died that I wish I had known when they were alive." When a minister visits a family after a death, especially where there has been little previous contact, you learn a great deal about the person who has died. I visited Cyril Flint in hospital the week before he died and quickly discovered that we had much in common.

Roots in the north-east where he had been brought up in New Delaval, Blyth. We talked about sport and the forthcoming Charity Shield game. A lifelong Newcastle United supporter, linking through the YMCA with George Robledo and thrilling to the exploits of "Wor Jackie" Milburn, Cyril was daft about sport. A football referee-you have to be a bit daft to be one of those! He represented Northumberland County at flat-green bowls, but could not bring himself to play what he called the "humpty back" bowls so popular in this area. Playing tennis, took him regularly to Wimbledon and playing snooker, to Sheffield for several world finals, as a spectator I hasten to add. A speedway supporter for over 40 years of Newcastle Diamonds in younger days and Belle Vue aces while living here, he was also the proud father as son Graham qualified last year as the youngest ever Speedway Referee. Like me, Cyril began work as a civil servant. **The Ministry of Pensions, National Service in the RAF, and for 37 years with what was originally Post Office Telephones and is now British Telecom.**

I am grateful to Post Office Telephones for my basic training in office administration and customer relations, but I can only imagine the kind of changes that Cyril had to cope with over a lifetime of work there.

The beginnings of change were there in the 1960's when Cyril and Margaret moved to this area, but it rattled on apace as public concern gave way to privatization and profits.

Margaret and Cyril can thank Post Office Telephones for bringing them together. Well, Post Office Telephones and Cyril's motorbike which gave him an excuse for offering her a lift home. I do wonder what conversations they must have both had working together at British Telecom. Personally, I'm sure that you could have run it better as a partnership rather than a privatized company!

Fortunately, Cyril and Margaret's life did not have to focus around work. They became members of the church here in the 70's- Cyril reckoned that he converted Margaret from C of E. If that was the case, Margaret had her revenge by roping Cyril in to share much of her work with the Girls Brigade.

Cyril became a Communion Steward, a Door Steward, and with his accounts background the Treasurer of the Contact Magazine. The church meant a great deal to Cyril, and people here were a great support when their son William died in a road accident 9 years ago. Death is no stranger to this family.

At any funeral service we learn something of the person who has died, but in this case we learn too of how lessons learned about God in and through tragedy help us all to be renewed in our faith. For conversation about the person who has died turns naturally to questions about death.

Margaret and I were able to share with each other some things that we have learned. Two or three of those thoughts we share with you all.

The only real clues that help us answer the question, "Why God?" that we ask about suffering and death are to be found in the sacrificial death of Jesus on a cross.

The message of love's death on a cross is followed by the victory over death evidenced in the empty tomb.

The clear teaching of Jesus about eternal life is enshrined in Jn. 5.24 "I am telling you the truth: whoever hears my words and believes in him who has sent me has eternal life. He will not be judged, but has already passed from death to life." Eternal life does not begin when we die, it begins when we believe, when we come to faith in Jesus Christ. There's a lovely and I think a most helpful phrase used in the New Testament of those who die in Christ.

The scriptures talk about the believer as "falling asleep" in Christ. The child falls asleep in his father's arms. Now I can cope with that, "Falling asleep in Christ". (AV & RSV) 1 Cor 15: 6 & 18)

Cyril believed and has simply "Fallen asleep in Christ". We who live on must learn to live in Christ that we may rest assured that we shall die in Christ.

Let's hear the Apostle Paul explain it to us in 1 Cor 15:6

"Then he appeared to more than five hundred brethren at one time, most of whom are still alive, though some have fallen asleep."

So, we sing,

**LORD JESUS CHRIST,
YOU HAVE COME TO US....
RISEN FROM DEATH TO SET US FREE;
LIVING LORD JESUS, HELP US SEE
YOU ARE LORD.**

HALFORD: Ian died 5th August 1994 aged 53

When certain churches are having difficulty with allowing "dad" and "granddad" on gravestones, I wonder how they would cope with, "A Big Softie" on the headstone. **"A Big Softie", the family's affectionate description of Ian, says much about the man.** Ian Halford spent much of his life in the competitive world of the fashion business and it showed. It showed on the outside in the flamboyance and flare of one who loved clothes. The picture that will remain in the mind of those who saw only the outside is of Ian, immaculately dressed and as stiff as the shirt much beloved of his father and lovingly ironed and starched by his mother. A "dandy" is "one who affects special finery in dress". Ian was not a "dandy" in the true sense of the word because his dress was not an affectation, but an expression of the kind of person that he was whether dressing, catering or caring.

In some ways the private person was protected in business by the outward appearance, but the "big softie" soon came to the fore in situations where people knew him and he them. The T.V. series, "Are you being Served" had nothing on some of the tall tales told of dealing with customers. A particularly awkward customer went to change into a new pair of trousers. On returning he observed, "People are looking in your changing room window", to which Ian replied, "Don't worry sir, its mirror glass, no one can see in." Perhaps Ian was too soft-centred to succeed as the world deems success in business, but there are countless tales told of his simple, "cup of tea" kindness to the many different people with whom he came into contact. It was that inherent kindness that made him valued as a good friend by so many outside the world of work, Ian's great love was for his family. Nurtured himself with his much-loved brother Brian. (even Biblical brothers had their upsets, Brian) in a Christian home.

His mother Irene had a Quaker background; perhaps that's where he learned his quietness: His father as a Baptist lay preacher would share both the conviction and the commitment of a different generation.

Ian and Muriel together translated that background into a fresh environment within which their own children, David, Sarah and Fiona have been nurtured in Christian values. Once again, in family life, the fun-loving father belied the public image. "The Big Softie" was devoted to Muriel, his wife, and would do anything for his family. A promotion and the consequent move at work was assessed by how much it would benefit the family. Family occasions like Sarah and James's wedding last year were a great joy to Ian, but personally I love the story of Ian and Muriel sitting down for a celebration drink at midnight when David & Carol had "done their own thing" and gone off to get married in Las Vegas. Ian lifting his glass and humorously complaining to Muriel, "What a way to celebrate my only son's wedding!" His pride in his family is matched by theirs in him. As a father Ian was good in relating to his own children and their friends as individuals in their own right. As a grandfather he was just besotted.

Nathan literally translated from the Hebrew is "He has given". Nathan, born to Fiona in January was received as God's gift to the whole family, but he became also a fresh focus for Ian's love. The balance of discipline and love that is the lot of any good father gave way to the unrestrained love that doting grand-parents are allowed. "The Big Softie" was in his element as he lavished his love and shared playfully with the latest addition to the Halford clan. Nathan of the Bible was the prophet whose gentle story of the rich man taking advantage of the poor man in 2 Sam 12 convicted King David of his sin in taking another man's wife. Every man of God, like Nathan, shares with us something of God's attitude towards people. So, God our Father does not hesitate to confront us when we are doing wrong and challenge us to do right. God, our Father, balances his law with his love and gets alongside us through the example of Jesus and the presence of the Holy Spirit to encourage us to live in his way. Ian shared something of God with us.

God too is a "Big Softie" at heart, wanting to share his love with the world. Our prayer is that you will have that assurance of his love in your world today.

HALL: Gwynneth died 21ˢᵗ August 1992 aged 82

I suppose the best known and perhaps the most loved passage of scripture is the 23rd. Psalm, "The Lord is my shepherd, I shall not want." Certainly, set to the tune Crimond, it is the most used hymn in funeral services for church-goers and non-church-goers alike. Apart from that hymn there are two other favourite hymns in our hymn book based on the 23rd. Psalm. "In Heavenly Love Abiding, No Change My Heart Shall Fear" and the one that Gwynneth Hall chose, "THE KING OF LOVE MY SHEPHERD IS", but more of that in a moment.

Gwynn Hall was born in the year that gave birth to the Girl Guide movement. The scouts had been founded by Baden-Powell three years earlier. One wonders whether Frank and Gwynn would have been brought together without the help of Baden-Powell. The Rover-Scout and the Ranger-Guide did come together and from that time marriage and the family that blossomed from it became the focus of Gwynn's life. Early association with church and Sunday School gave way to looking after her own Sunday School of four children and an extended family of husbands and wives with ten grandchildren.

Gwynn, basically a shy person, was a follower rather than a leader in most situations, but that did not stop her making her own contribution to the care of babies at the Brookdale Clinic and helping back up the work of the Mary Dendy unit for handicapped youngsters at Alderley Edge. Charities for children like the N.S.P.C.C. benefitted from her work and she was ready to help the church with its magazine distribution network. The Rover-Scout Frank's enthusiasm for the great outdoors has not waned, but Ranger-Gwynn was determined not to be left behind. Walking, camping and climbing Helvellyn at the age of 52 was proof enough of that determination. Nevertheless, whatever Gwynn did, it came second to her love and concern for Frank and the family. Perhaps, it was that love of family that made her such an avid watcher of soaps on T.V. in later years and Coronation Street in particular. The addictive quality of soaps is bound up with family lives and illustrated in the hype that surrounds the weddings of the characters that take part.

It was not the hyped-up wedding of a soap, but the real wedding of her grandson David that was to be the finale before the curtain came down on Gwynn's life. Ill-health had not sapped her determination to be there to celebrate with her beloved family that final family occasion. It is always interesting in Christian terms to examine a person's choice of hymns, for it so often sums up their faith. "The King of Love My Shepherd Is", translates the Old Testament terminology of the Shepherd Psalm into New Testament language. The Jehovah Lord of the O.T. becomes the King of Love in the N.T. The pastoral "Still waters" become the life-giving streams of living water. The fourth verse introduces the cross, the symbol of sacrificial love alongside the rod and staff that comfort, and the fifth verse links the table with the communion in which we celebrate what God has done for us in Jesus Christ. Central to this hymn are the words of verse three which relate to the parable of the lost sheep in Luke chapter 15. **Perverse and foolish oft I strayed, but yet in love he sought me, and on his shoulder gently laid, and home rejoicing brought me.**

God's love for us is mirrored in Gwynn's love for her family. No family is held together over so many years without some regrets. It's God's love and forgiveness that deals with any regrets, for he seeks us all in the same way as the shepherd cares for the lost sheep. The author of this hymn Sir Henry Baker, as he lay dying at the age of 56, was heard quietly repeating these words, "Perverse and foolish, oft I strayed". Perhaps Gwynn did at times too. The hope of the Old Testament. "Surely goodness and mercy shall follow me", becomes in this hymn a prayer of assurance that all who live in God's love can sing, "And so through all the length of days thy goodness faileth never; Good Shepherd, may I sing thy praise within thy house for ever. The King. of love is the one on whom we all depend at this time. **I trust that something of Gwynn's faith that prompted the choice of this hymn will bring comfort as we sing her chosen hymn,**

"The King of love, my Shepherd is, whose goodness faileth never;
 I nothing lack if I am his and he is mine forever."

HARRIS: Margaret E. died 10th December 1993 aged 73

I continue to be surprised as a minister when I begin to delve into people's background in preparation for a funeral service. People who you think that you know fairly well, you discover you hardly knew at all and people like Margaret Harris who you have known only as a rather frail elderly person turn out to have been involved in much more than you imagine in their younger days.

Margaret was born in Essex and survived the London bombing raids in Ilford. The one bombshell that hit her was Jack. They were married during the war but it was not until 1964 that they moved to this area to live in Woodford. Who would have thought that the frail body whom many in this church came to know only in recent years: combined being a skilled painter of decorative plates, and a dog breeder, with the more normal activities of gardening, handiwork, sewing and the like? Margaret was an outgoing person who enjoyed social activities. She was the kind of person who could sit on a bus and be in conversation with someone within minutes. She was a long-time member of the Women's Institute at Woodford Community Centre and in the past few years loved to join in with Pop-in and the Tuesday Fellowship in this church. Even when she was not well, she kept going and couldn't wait to be back amongst the many friends that she had made. Strangely enough, it was perhaps this more than anything else that led to some improvement in her health as Robert brought her into Centrepoint most mornings for coffee. The general improvement there had been in her health, made it a greater shock when she died suddenly last week.

There is always a particular sadness when people die close to Christmas. When others are enjoying the run up to and the family celebration of Christmas, it seems for the family who have lost a loved one at this time that every Christmas from then on will be tinged with sad memories. That may be true for those who live with no hope. For the Christian there is a plus side in that throughout the whole of Advent and indeed at Christmas itself we are surrounded by reminders of God's love for the world. Cards and Christmas trees with Christian symbols tell of a divine love that is neither trivialized nor commercialized by all the trimmings. The carols that we sing ring out with praise of a God who cared enough for this world to send his only Son to live and die for those of us who live in it. Even the countless meals and mince pies that older folk are invited to at this time are an expression of the love of God for all. Perhaps we have yet one more important thing to learn about Margaret at this time.

Margaret loved to be pushed through into this church in her wheelchair and simply sit and soak up the atmosphere, to sense the presence of God. It was here in the quietness, surrounded by those things that reminded her of God, that she found her faith renewed sufficiently to cope with her deteriorating health. Margaret was a lively person who loved lively music and an active social life. It is perhaps significant that renewal came for her in the silence as she contemplated the things of God. It may well be that there is a lesson in this for all of us caught up in the hurly-burly associated with the preparation for Christmas, that there is a place of quiet and peace to be found here where God can share his peace and love with us. I, personally, am pleased that Jack and Robert have chosen one of our favourite Advent hymns for this service.

It will help us to reflect on how the fact that Margaret's death is so close to Christmas allows us to use the message of Advent as a source of comfort in our sadness. Hear and take to heart the words of:

Come, thou long expected Jesus,
Born to set thy people free,
From our fears and sins release us,
Let us find our rest in thee

Our prayer is that Jack, Robert and all those who are saddened by the loss of a loved one at this time may quietly reflect on the reminders of God's love that surround us in Advent/Christmas.

And like Margaret herself, be renewed to live or die assured of the love of God expressed in Jesus Christ.

HINSLEY: Ida died 27th August 1994 aged 73

Only very close friends would trace the connection between Ida Hinsley and "short, fat, hairy legs." Yes, Ida was one of the millions of people who loved to watch Morecombe & Wise. Their typically British slapstick humour allowed Ida to forget her pain-racked body and enjoy such lines as, "What do you think of it so far? Rubbish!" Lest she be saying the same thing about this address, I had better make clear why I begin with this thought. Ida, even when she was crippled with creeping and cruel arthritis, came across as someone who enjoyed life and was interested in people. Those of us who only knew Ida in her later years have to imagine a very different person in her youth. Born in the 1920's Ida's early years were moulded in a country and a part of Manchester suffering the consequences of economic depression. Her own working life would see her involved in the most unlikely activities. Office work yes, but who would have thought that the frail body that I came to know was once a much larger stronger lady who was at home in a workshop handling, or should I say manhandling, both light and heavy engineering.

Ida's real introduction to Methodism was in the early 40's when she became a member of the Albert Hall in Manchester. Membership alone was not sufficient for this enthusiastic young woman; she then became a missionary. Yes, a missionary of the kind seen much more frequently in those days than in the present. A missionary is one who goes out from their own settled situation into a culture or situation not their own to share something of Jesus Christ. Ida responded to an appeal for Sunday school teachers at the Raby Street Methodist Church in the Moss Side area of Manchester where the foundations were laid for her life-long friendship with Clarice. After a long spell teaching in the Primary and Junior Departments at Raby Street that church closed and Ida moved on again with pupils and staff to the Great Western Street Church. In addition, Clarice and Ida were loaned to the Claremont Road Sunday School to assist the severely depleted staff build up numbers in the period immediately after the war. Hundreds of youngsters were influenced by her work in the Sunday School. Both she and Clarice rejoiced to hear about those special ones who went on to become a full-time missionary of the more traditional kind overseas. Ida was a born organiser and was in her element whether preparing the children for Sunday School Anniversaries, planning the old Rose Queen Festivals, arranging flowers in bouquets, or directing a concert party which helped to raise funds for the church. It didn't really matter whether you were a child or an adult, Ida organised you!

Long before the advent of computers Ida had a mind that worked like one. Diary dates, birthdays, anniversaries and happenings that affected people were recalled without difficulty. It takes more than a computer though to use such a gift as Ida did to express love and concern for others through such attention to detail. Sadly, Ida's health was already beginning to fail when Ida and Clarice came to Bramhall about 17 years ago. Attendance at Link and the Friday Club where she loved to meet people tailed off and getting to worship became difficult. Much enjoyed holidays overseas or walking in the Lake District were no more. Nevertheless, Ida maintained a lively interest in everything.

She was always thankful for all those friends who kept her in touch with life outside the walls of her flat. It would be invidious to name names other than Clarice on this occasion, but all of you will be aware of how grateful both Ida and Clarice have been for your practical friendship. There's a proverb that says, "The eyes are the window of the soul." Above all with Ida, I shall remember her eyes that seemed to grow larger as her body withered. The large brown eyes that filled with the excitement of a ride on a speed boat and with laughter at Clarice making the front page of the Daily Mirror (Clarice can explain that!) Those eyes continued to express in the words of the next hymn chosen from Ida's favourites, **"Joy that seekest me through pain."** Dr. Matheson, who wrote the hymn, once explained the "blossoms red" in the final verse. **"I took red as the symbol of that sacrificial life which had bloomed by shedding its life." White blossoms come from prosperity, red from sacrifice.**

It's Ida's joy won through sacrifice that we celebrate here today.

HORROBIN: James (Jim) died 20th Jan. 1996 aged 93

Jim Horrobin, born 24th Jan 1902. The date conjures up for me pictures of Queen Victoria who died on the 22nd Jan 1901 and images of the British Empire with its splashes of red on coloured maps that showed the extent of this nation's influence around the world. Jim Horrobin, born in Burnley, was British and he was proud of it. You couldn't be in conversation very long with Jim without realising how much his birth and beginnings provided a pattern for his life.

He wasn't quite born on a train, but as he shares in an article that he wrote for the journal of the Lancashire and Yorkshire Railway Society, the railways were in his blood. "My Father was one of two inspectors on the 'grids'. Father's younger brother, Thomas, was agent at Todmorden and Accrington. Mother's brother, Henry Hindle, was Chief Staff Clerk. Grandfather was a freight guard. Two cousins were relief clerks and one sister in the Audit Dept at Hunts Bank." As Jim himself said in the article, "So it was inevitable, my destination was the L &Y Railway."

What was not inevitable was the deep love for everything to do with railways that grew from the time he began as a clerk at the age of 14 on the L & Y Railway. I haven't time this morning to share with you everything in the article, but I think that this extract talks not only of very different days, but shares something of Jim's humour. "My first week was 2/6, retained by the company in case of AWL, the second was 5/-, including 2/6 war bonus. We had an excellent dining room at Hunts Bank, subsidised by the company. A full course dinner was 1/- per day, so I worked a week for five dinners." L & Y, Lancashire & Yorkshire, LMS, London Midland & Scottish, all sounds so much more romantic than British Rail from which Jim retired officially at 60, but continuing to work as needed on special projects for another five years. Retirement came and went, but Jim's interest in and love affair with the railways never waned. His work had become his leisure.

Any conversation on romance and love relating to railways would be overshadowed by thoughts of Jim's beloved wife Nellie. His own settled family background as the youngest of three children with two older sisters, Edith & Sadie (who is still alive) had prepared him well for marriage. I'm not sure that Jim realised that he would have to court Nellie for ten years until he was 29 and she 25 before Nellie's mother thought she was old enough to be married and their family could do without her income. Jim thought it was well worth the wait. Jim and Nellie married in 1931 at Failsworth Wesleyan Chapel and set up house in a two-up, two-down cottage built by Nellie's grandfather a few doors down from Nellie's parents. It was there that Bill, Michael and Margaret were born, before they moved to Hartington Road in Bramhall in 1938. The family was to remain in Bramhall till the late 60's when Jim and Nellie moved in retirement to North Wales, an area they had always loved.

Their love affair continued in a new setting until Nellie died quite suddenly in 1987. Her death was in some ways the beginning of the end too for Jim. He struggled on in North Wales until he returned to Bramhall in 1993 to live with Bill & Pam. Jim appreciated the love and concern of all his family. He was thankful for the practical and costly caring of Bill and Pam, particularly after he came to live with them as ill health dogged his final years, but the light of his life went out with the death of Nellie. He was full of memories and loved to talk about her with those who knew her as old friends in Bramhall visited him.

The third love of Jim's life was his church. A lifelong Wesleyan-not I think just because he met Nellie at Failsworth Wesleyan church-though he was in the Boy Scouts with her older brothers Robert and Wallace and played a lot of snooker with them. Jim had a deep faith in God and a lasting commitment to his church which saw him serve the church wherever he lived. Even in the later years at Llandudno he was active in the choir at St. David's Methodist Church.

During the thirty years that he, Nellie, and the family lived in Bramhall, Jim served the church in a variety of ways. He sang in the choir became a Society Steward and in turn a Circuit Steward. Jim was deeply committed to his church and his Lord. Like so many Methodists of earlier generations his hymn book was his prayer book. In the last few months as I shared communion with Jim at Bill and Pam's we would begin with me asking Jim for a hymn. No hymn book was necessary as Jim recited the words of a different hymn every time.

Jim was conscious of his own failures in living and loving and in those acts of Communion with God he sought the forgiveness of anyone whom he had hurt as he grew increasingly impatient with the restrictions imposed by ill health and old age.

Despite his own admitted faults the three loves of his life, his work, his wife and family, and his faith had kept the old railwayman on the right track. Nearing the end, the church choir stalwart found the hymn book best expressed his feelings and his faith. It seems so appropriate now that our Pastor Chris Cowlishaw was able to discern a response from Jim, as, last Saturday morning, just before he died Chris spoke the words,

> "How sweet the name of Jesus sounds
> In a believer's ear!
> It soothes his sorrows, heals his wounds,
> And drives away his fear."

I'm sure that Jim would accept the words of John Newton's hymn as his life's testimony. So, we sing the hymn 257 in celebration of Jim's life and use the final verse to refresh our own faith and trust in God.

> **"Till then I would thy love proclaim**
> **With every fleeting breath;**
> **And may the music of thy name**
> **refresh my soul in death."**

HOUGH: H. Marjorie died 5th June 1993 aged 76

Sybil Hall has spoken for us all in what she has shared about Marjorie Hough. I would like to pick up where she left off, not so much with the person, but with the faith in Jesus Christ that Marjorie demonstrated in a very real way. Whenever I went to see Marjorie even in the last few months when she herself was so unwell, she always enquired after other people. Marjorie had hoped that Harry Robinson would play the hymns that she had chosen at her funeral service, but alas Harry was one of whom she enquired who was to go on ahead of her. In preparing for today and with two funeral services in the one week I realised afresh how many deaths our church has had to cope with in recent months. All of them faithful members who have joined the Church Triumphant, but continue in fellowship with us.

Near the end of our Communion Service, we say these words:
"We thank you, Lord that you have fed us in this sacrament, united us with Christ, and given us a foretaste of the heavenly banquet prepared for all mankind." True fellowship with other people on earth is always a "foretaste of the fellowship of Heaven." though it may not seem like it at times. If we were to spend time this morning remembering all those people whom we have loved and lost, we would realise that our memories have made saints of them all. Not that any of them were perfect-that's left to us to think that we are that, but we recognise in the lives of each one something of what Margaret read for us from Paul's letter to Corinth. **"These three remain: faith, hope and love; and the greatest of these is love."**

Love is the one thing that lasts forever. Paul is talking about human love being expressed in practical ways, but if you were to read that passage again tonight and put the word God before each mention of the word love, you will be reminded of one of the two important reasons why Christians believe that death is not the end. Love lasts for ever, whether it's God's love or our own. We know that is true from our own human experience of personal relationships. At the core of every expression of friendship/fellowship is love.

When we repeat the benediction, "the Grace of our Lord Jesus Christ, the Love of God and the Fellowship of the Holy Spirit" we are saying that God loves us in three different ways, but all of those ways will last for ever.

The second reason why Christians believe in life after death is because Jesus in the passage that we have just read says we should. Communion is not a foretaste of the heavenly banquet prepared for all mankind simply because we share it with each other. Our sharing now and in the life to come is in the presence of one, Jesus Christ, who demonstrated for all time that his words were true by being raised from the dead. Martyrs down the ages have lived and died for that truth. Paul said, "For me to die is gain." Dietrich Bonhoeffer the Christian pastor executed by the Nazis in 1945 in his last words to his friends said, "This is the end, for me the beginning of life." Marjorie like so many of those who have died in recent months has suffered so much and yet her faith shone through. A faith that did not rest on her feelings, which could be pretty down at times, but a faith in the Lord Jesus Christ who has paved the way through suffering and death for all of us who believe in him.

We are faced with a choice in our attitude to death. Like the sad philosopher Bertrand Russell we can believe, "There is darkness without, and when I die there will be darkness within. There is no splendour, no vastness anywhere; only triviality for the moment, and then nothing." Personally, the splendour of our friends' living and the courage and confidence with which they have died has made me surer than ever that the promise of Jesus is true, "Where I am, you may be also." Our fellowship **WITH THEM** and our faith **IN HIM** is summed up in our final hymn:

> **Lord of the living, in your name assembled,**
> **We join to thank you for the life remembered.**
> **Lord, you can lift us from the grave of sorrow**
> **Into the presence of your own tomorrow;**
> **Give to your people for the day's affliction**
> **Your benediction.**

JOHNSON: Anthony (Tony) died 12th Sept. 1994 aged 50

From what I have learned about Tony Johnson over the past couple of weeks the last thing that he would want is to have some minister who didn't know him up here pretending that he was some kind of a saint. Nevertheless, any minister worth his salt must take account of the kind of things that family and friends say about a person who has died. Tony Johnson was above all a family man who loved Poll and his children as much as they loved him. The perfectionist in Tony came out as he renovated their home at Gawsworth Close for the family from top to bottom on their move from Cheadle Heath. I don't know of any large family that stays as close as this one has without a great deal of give and take. I'm sure that the Johnson family has had its fair share of problems, but the way in which they have dealt with them can be summed up in Poll's lovingly and humorously expressed words to Tony, "You're a pig." When that is reinforced by the present of a pink, fluffy pig, it says it all. Both Tony and Pauline lived in large families and learned how to live and love together.

Obviously, Tony wasn't a saint. He couldn't be. He supported Manchester City-but then again you have to be some kind of saint to support them! No, Tony was just an ordinary bloke who worked hard In Fabrics at Setcrepes, Portwood, and later with Sovereign Rubber in Hillgate. He enjoyed his pint at the Vic and even more when it was accompanied by a Saturday night victory over the younger generation at snooker. He enjoyed the humour of Benny Hill, Blackadder and was one of those who didn't need an interpreter for the accent of Rab C Nesbitt. They were the fun programmes on T.V., but the family knew not to disturb Tony when he was watching the serious stuff-football and sport in general. For an ordinary man, who to the outsider might have given the impression of being totally self-confident, Tony was extraordinarily sensitive as to what other people thought. He could be easily hurt by the comments that other people made and he went out of his way not to upset the neighbours. There was some insecurity there that had Tony feeling much more comfortable when he was on home ground, among friends or with the family who loved him. All of you will have your own memories of Tony and will fill in the background to what I have said with your own thoughts. But, you know, it doesn't really matter what any of you thought of Tony now-what really matters is what God thinks of Tony and what you think of God.

Tony wasn't a church-goer, as you well know, but from the moment that Mark, out of his family's love for their Father came to share his concerns in this church, Tony was incorporated into the prayer and worship life of this place. We, almost as much as the family were praying that Tony would come through his operation and be restored to his family. It was not to be and we as a church, like the family, question, "Why God, why?" None of us will ever know the answer to that in this life. What I do know and share with you now is that if death is just a dead end, then life is a meaningless farce. The Bible insists, "love never ends" and I for one cannot believe that the kind of love shared within the Johnson family has not had within it something of the love of God. Now is not the time to enter into a theological debate about life after death, but those who would deny it need to face up to the consequences of such a dead end philosophy here and now. Personally, I would far rather put my faith in the one whose words we have been reading, Jesus Christ the Son of God, who promised even the penitent thief on the Cross, "Today, you shall be with me in Paradise." What matters now is not what you think about Tony, but what you think about God. In a few moments we shall be singing an unusual hymn for a funeral which in the chorus repeats,

> **"All things bright and beautiful,**
> **All creatures great and small,**
> **All things wise and wonderful,**
> **The Lord God made them all."**

God made us all and anyone's death reminds us that we too have to die. Tony has gone to the God who made him: by his death we who live on are given the opportunity to come to know God so well in this life that we shall have no fear for Tony or ourselves in the next.

JONES: Edna M. died 11th July 1993 aged 72

I was going to begin by apologising for the clutter of the Flower Festival preparations that surround us, but I realised that it seems entirely appropriate for the funeral service of Edna Jones. Edna was one of those who had offered to help with the Festival and would have been sharing in these preparations. She was also the kind of person who spent her life doing, at just such an occasion as this. If there were practical things to be done or coffee to be made Edna would make herself available. Even when she was not feeling well herself, she would be on duty on one of the many rotas for coffee mornings or Tuesday Fellowship. It didn't matter whether it was the church, the British Legion, from whom she received an award for services rendered, or the Hillbrook Grange Fayre, Edna was at the front of the queue of willing helpers in practical service.

Seventy-two years ago, Edna Jones was born on the Wirral. She learned to share and to serve others as one of seven children brought up in West Kirby. She moved to Bramhall just after the war in 1946 and has lived in Moreton Avenue ever since. Her strong Christian faith undergirded her life and sustained her in the loss of her husband, Jack, some years ago. In some ways she was a very private person, but the welcoming smile on her face made her seem much less reserved than might have been the case. To put it simply, she was just a lovely Christian lady. My memory of Edna will be of a quiet lady who willingly and cheerfully served others in whatever way she could, but as a minister I sometimes wonder at the devoted service that people give and feel for words that will be an encouragement to the rest of us at a time such as this.

Today, I have been helped by Edna's family who have shared with me a verse that epitomises Edna's attitude to life. I share it with you now.

Do not make a hardship of the things you have to do.
Don't regard them as a bore, it all depends on you.

Whether you enjoy your work or whether it's a strain,
you make your own conditions by the thoughts inside your brain.
It's your mental attitude, yourself, your frame of mind,
Some folks let things weigh them down and others are inclined,
To take a different point of view and do with willing hands,
all the little things that go to make up life's demands.
Do not frown or make a fuss or grumble at your lot,
if there's something to be done then do it on the spot.
Welcoming the chance to do a service great or small,
isn't that just what you're put on earth for, after all.

Edna never made a great fuss about her Christian faith, but the family have chosen an appropriate hymn in "Abide with me." The hymn was written by Henry Francis Lyte, a Church of England vicar who knew that he was dying. He drew inspiration from the story of the two disciples who walked to Emmaus on that first Easter Day. They failed to recognise Jesus, but said, "Abide with us; for it is toward evening and the day is far spent." In this hymn Henry Lyte is talking about the eventide of his own life and wondering how to meet the end. The whole hymn takes the form of an intensely personal prayer with the repeated plea "Abide with me." The Hymn offers no easy answers to the problems of suffering and death, but it simply assumes the abiding presence of Jesus Christ in all the circumstances of life. This was an assumption that Edna Jones lived by.

As we sing this hymn, we share her faith. The original words of the final verse when written were not as printed here:

"Shine through the gloom," but "Speak through the gloom,"

Who can doubt that God had spoken to Edna Jones? Certainly, her faith allowed her to sing with confidence, "In life, in death, O Lord, abide with me." That same confidence allows us to sing:

Hold thou thy cross before my closing eyes;
Shine through the gloom, and point me to the skies;
Heaven's morning breaks and earth's vain shadows flee;
In life, in death, O Lord, abide with me!

LYON: Ruth died 25th September 1994 aged 79

Ruth Lyon was born on St Valentine's day in 1915. The patron saint of lovers seems to have influenced her life ever since. As a youngster the lively and good-looking Ruth had no problem making friends in the place where she was brought up-God's own country: Stockton-On-Tees. The family moved to Beswick when Ruth was eleven, but her social life continued to be bound up with the Methodist Church to which she gave a lifetime of service. As for so many people in those days the church was more than a place to worship. It was a school for life, a community centre and a place for practising relationship skills, all rolled into one.

Ruth practiced her relationship skills freely until she met her husband-to-be Frank through the Boys Brigade of the Beswick Methodist Church. She ran the Primary Sunday School, played the organ for church services and played the piano for all kinds of events. Between her and son Howard they managed to collect for the Junior Missionary Association for well over thirty years-they have the medals to prove it. Ruth with a mop and bucket boarding a bus and heading for a clean-up of the church was a sight to behold. Outside church, Ruth worked as an eiderdown cutter with her sister Lily and she married Frank just before the war. Her love for her own parents and sister Lily was now matched by a deep love for Frank, their only child Howard, and subsequently, his wife Jill, their children and Ruth's grandchildren Andrew and Kathryn. Pride in, "Our Howard", became pride in their family and Howard, despite his cricketing exploits, now had to compete for the limelight with Andrew and Kathryn.

It was the love at the very centre of this family's life that eventually drew Ruth and Frank away from their beloved Beswick Methodist Church to find their home close to Howard and Jill in Bramhall and as part of the fellowship of this church. Ruth rarely enjoyed the best of health and after continuing problems the decision was made to move here in 1970. Frank died just three years later, but the move allowed the family to be together.

St. Valentine came to the fore again as her love of life, of her church and ordinary people touched the lives of so many. It didn't matter whether it was the minister with his weakness for Kit-Kats, or the stranger nervously popping her head around the door of the crush hall, Ruth knew just the right approach to make people feel welcome. Ruth once again became totally involved in the life of the church, attending Link Meetings and playing the piano for the Tuesday Fellowship, but her most valuable work to my mind was as part of the small group of older members that we affectionately call the 'Youth Group' who sat inside the Crush Hall doors, drinking coffee and indulging in people spotting. "Richard", she would say, "do you know so and so?" Many of those "so and so's" spotted and welcomed by Ruth are now members of this church and some are present with us today.

From her birth on St. Valentine's day, through to her familiar greeting, "Hello love". Ruth's life was an expression of God's love. Ruth was also a grateful person and she would not want me to let this occasion pass without an expression of her gratitude for the love and care that has been lavished upon her by so many people. The evergreen Lily has borne the brunt, ably supported by Fred, and all of them have been cared for by Howard, Jill and the family. It would be invidious to pick out others, but let the unnamed former Primary School scholar of Ruth's who came to her hospital bedside not too long ago stand for all of us in receiving Ruth's thanks for love returned in practical expressions of caring.

Born on St. Valentine's Day, Ruth's funeral service is held today on the feast of St. Michael. St. Michael was regarded as a special protector of the sick and in some traditions is regarded as the receiver of the souls of the dead. As a dyed-in-the-wool Methodist, I'm not sure that Ruth would approve of being linked to so many saints. She would approve of being linked with "living in love", despite the sickness, as a reminder that testified to God's strength and a faith that would see death as St. Michael simply:

"Rowing the boat ashore" with her in it, to land peacefully in the presence of a loving God on that other shore.

McNEIL: Bessie M. died early December 1993

What does it take to foster 100 children and to bring up two families of your own?

An abundance of love and a great deal of determination.

Love and determination were qualities that made Bessie McNeil the kind of person that she was.

Those of us who have had to cope with the temperament and teenage tantrums of a couple of children of our own can only marvel at someone like Bessie. Four children in her first marriage, Barry, Tony, Angela and John. Three children, Pam, Janet and Sandy from her second marriage and then because she had time on her hands as her own children grew up, she took on responsibility for fostering this large number of youngsters. Youngsters coming from all kinds of family backgrounds and situations; some with personal problems to be coped with, others who simply needed the security that being loved gives.

What a testimony to Bessie's love and determination that not one of the youngsters who came to her ever ended up in a care home. Some returned to their natural parents, better able to cope, others were adopted and yet others became part of Bessie's own extended family.

A brief look at Bessie's background gives some clues as to how she was brought up to be mum to so many. She was the oldest daughter of ten children, born in Murrow, Wisbech St Mary in Cambridgeshire. She was proud of the fact that her father was a Methodist Local Preacher and her up-bringing in a Christian home was to stand her in good stead throughout her life. From that large family she "went into service", lovely old phrase that, in St Albans at the age of 14.

As a child in such a large family and "in service" Bessie learned how to cope easily with the domestic tasks that were part and parcel of her life at that time. The death of her own mother when Bessie was only thirty years of age meant that her own family too looked upon the oldest daughter as a substitute mum.

Two marriages that produced seven children, but did not last, taught Bessie how to survive the ups and downs of life and her family endured with her hard, but happy childhoods. It's a tribute to Bessie's ability to make ends meet that none of her children felt deprived as the secure marriage relationships which she would have loved disintegrated around her.

Thankfully, Bessie's background gave her an inner security which communicated itself to her own family and to all the youngsters for whom she became responsible at crisis stages in their lives. I was reminded of a phrase from the Falkland Islands crisis when the family described how their Saturday visits to mum were almost logged in her mind. Each member of her extended family was special to Bessie, She "counted them all out, and counted them all back." And there was always a meal on the table.

Her love and determination never faltered as her later years were dogged by ill-health. Those who knew her well would not be surprised at her tackling a trip to Australia in a wheelchair just six years ago. Going to see her family there was a highlight of her later years and the memory was kept alive as she shared with her visitors reminders of that very special holiday.

You can't imagine such an active person being happy with the inactivity brought on by illness and old age, and she wasn't. She appreciated the loving care of family and close friends, and the nursing care provided at Marple Dale, but the mother on whom so many depended found it hard to be dependent. A difficult lesson to learn for older people.

As I read the scriptures and prayed with Bessie on the day before she died, I knew very little about her.

Brought up in a Christian home, linked with churches in Wisbech and here with the Offerton Methodist Church, she wasn't able to talk about her faith to me.

The family says of her that she was the tree and all the family were branches. From what I have heard of Bessie since, I can only believe that the roots that nurtured the tree were deep into the God whom she worshipped and prayed to.

The love and determination demonstrated in Bessie's life characterised the life of Jesus Christ. He was her example and she would want him to be yours. Hear His words to you.

The third verse of, "Away in a Manger", could have been Bessie's daily prayer and may serve as her epitaph today.

Be near me, Lord Jesus; I ask thee to stay
Close by me for ever, and love me, I pray.
Bless all the dear children in thy tender care,
And fit us for heaven, to live with thee there.

McQUILLAN: Alex(Zander) died 20th May 1996 aged 60

Just four weeks ago Zander McQuillan was here at the front of this church being prayed for at the beginning of his four-year term as a Steward of this church. Now we gather together in worship, shocked and saddened by our loss. Zander would have made an excellent Church Steward and he was proud to have been invited to serve God and the church in this way.

He would have made an excellent Church Steward because of his family background and experience at work. Born in 1935 and brought up with his older brother Bill by the sea in Portobello, the family moved to live in Edinburgh towards the end of the war. At an early age he betrayed his life-long concern for the underprivileged by joining the family at the nearby Easter Road ground and becoming a Hibs supporter!!! The brass band at half time might have kept him going! Hibs were always his team and people knew it.

Zander was educated in Edinburgh, going on from the Royal High School to the University where he became Dr. Alexander Hunter McQuillan in 1960 after completing his research in Radiation Chemistry.

Zander always felt that the more important of the titles that he earned about that time was that of a married man. Norma and Zander met as teenage youngsters through the Lockhart Memorial Church, but canny Scot that he was it took him a few years to get round to proposing! They married on the 8th May 1960. After a short time with the United Kingdom Atomic Energy Authority, Norma and Zander made the big move. They left family and friends behind in their beloved Scotland as Zander began his life's work with ICI based mainly at Runcorn. His valued expertise as a senior manager in almost thirty years of work with ICI at home and abroad would have brought invaluable experience into the Church Stewards team.

Zander would have made an excellent Church Steward because he was able to balance his enthusiasm for the work at ICI, which he enjoyed, with an even deeper commitment to Norma and his family. David was born in Helsby in 1964 and Claire at Chester in 1968. The family moved to Bramhall in 1972 when Zander was for a short time located with ICI Sales in Piccadilly Plaza in Manchester.

Rather than disturb the family again with yet another move, Zander continued to commute to Runcorn for the rest of his working life. Despite the pressures of business with long distance and international travel, Zander made time to be with Norma and the children. He even risked his life with Claire.

Driving down to Exeter with the newly qualified driver, he encouraged her to go a little faster than the 20 mph that she was travelling. His return by train was uneventful. When he did the same in reverse going down by train at the end of term to accompany the vastly experienced driver on her return, he vowed never again to sit in the front seat with her driving!

Zander's enjoyment of gardening and Do It Yourself held little attraction for the younger David, but more recent responsibilities have seen them sharing both these interests in David and Jayne's home. Zander was proud of his family. To see both David with Jayne, and newly engaged Claire with Philip in Hong Kong, settled and doing well, was a joy to Zander, but his greatest joy was to be found in a lifetime love affair with Norma.

Early retirement from ICI in 1988 simply served to provide fresh opportunities for them to be together doing those things that they loved to do. He treasured that time and the special love that they enjoyed in Christ. It was always Norma and Zander or Zander and Norma. The two became one in heart and mind.

Zander would have made an excellent Church Steward because he continued to grow in grace, good humour and in love for God. Norma and Zander have established links with churches throughout their married life and Zander gained valuable experience in church leadership and pastoral care as an elder of the United Reformed Church here in Bramhall.

As with so many of us, brought up in the church who become busy with work, family and doing, Zander's Christianity faced the danger of falling away into a kind of churchianity, where church going became more of a duty. Zander was saved from this by a deeply personal experience of God that came to him when facing a particularly difficult time at work.

That experience, retirement and a new commitment made during the Bramhall Christian Festival gave Zander and Norma a fresh enthusiasm for the things of God. They became members of this church in July 1992 and quickly became key workers as well as worshippers here. Their background in the URC and association with friends at Ford's Lane Evangelical Church have been invaluable ecumenical links as Zander became a moving force in establishing Christian Viewpoint for Men.

A common complaint about evangelicals is that, "They are so heavenly minded, that they are no earthly good." Zander was a practical man. He got his hands dirty in the church gardens and became an odd job man. Where others agonised about spending in well-off churches, Zander made a personal commitment to his own church alongside that made to needy churches like the Royal Thorn Evangelical Church in Wythenshawe and communities like Colshaw.

Even his smoking-not to be recommended even if the great preacher Spurgeon did indulge-allowed him to identify with unlikely people who on churchy occasions would pop out with him for a quick drag.

When we were looking for a new Chairman for the Centrepoint Advisory Council, it was Zander who stepped forward. Despite his strong views, he learned to laugh at himself and with other people. As one steward summed it up, "I liked Zander, he made me laugh!".

The practical man, the carer, the heart warmed by an evangelical spirit and the good humour combined together in Zander as he gave his all to the Alpha Course. Nothing gave him greater joy in the church over the past twelve months than to see men and women renewed in the faith and to hear new Christians giving testimony as to how their lives had been changed through participation in the Alpha Course. Yes, Zander would have made an excellent Church Steward.

But then, he did make an excellent steward of God's gifts to him in and through the church. The badge of office simply set the seal on his stewardship of many years. All of you present, all of what we have shared today is a testimony to his Christian Stewardship in every area of his life. Here's a description of Zander-you can find it in:

1 Tim 3.1-7 describing 'Leaders in the Church'.

"This is a true saying: If a man is eager to be a church leader, he desires an excellent work. A church leader must be without fault; he must have only one wife, be sober, self-controlled and orderly; he must welcome strangers in his home; he must be able to teach…….."

Zander was all of these things and we thank God for him. He was officially a Steward of this church for just one month, but Zander was Jesus Christ's Steward long before that.

He can wear his Bramhall Methodist Church's Stewards Badge with pride in heaven as he hears the commendation of Jesus:

"Well done, thou good and faithful servant!"

NEEDHAM: Bessie died 26th September 1988 aged 69

To hear someone say of Bessie, "The Church has been her whole life." might sound terribly boring to you if you have never known Bessie and the family. The Church was where the Needham family belonged. Bessie as a youngster was brought up in the Napier Street Methodist Church with the rest of her family. Belonging and sharing in the activities of the Sunday School and later the Youth Club was a natural progression towards joining more fully in the life of the church. Being part of the church was part of family life and when the dashing young Norman came along to carry her across the tracks to Wesley Street Methodist Church, it was just as natural that Bessie, Norman and Peter would become totally involved in all that was happening in and through that church. Bessie was the good lady behind the good Nor-man, supportive in everything from the Youth Club to the Dramatic Society. Very often it was Norman up front with Bessie as part of the catering corps without which Methodism would never survive, but together they were totally committed to a life of work and worship in and through the church.

The Church was where fun was found. The church in the Needham household has meant stoking old boilers (not preparing for the hereafter, though it may well have been mentioned) to vacating their home to make room for the Young People's Fellowship. They have been part of the Norbury Parish Bowling Society as well as Gilbert & Sullivan Concerts. Whether on holiday or at home, at work or in the garden, the church and what was needed there was never far from their thoughts.

The Church was where friendship was found. It took two years after Bessie and Norman's move to Bramhall before they could drag themselves away from the countless friends and families in their home church. It didn't take any time at all before they were well established with new friends and responsibilities associated with this Bramhall Methodist Church.

Bessie had faults and foibles like the best and rest of us, but above all she loved people, cared about them and it showed. Whether as Grandma Bessie in Playschool, Pop-in helper, Thrift Shop Worker, or Counsellor helping people through difficult times, Bessie cared. As the Epistle to James puts it, "She was a doer and not a hearer only"! Friends that she has made are now returning that love and friendship in support of Norman and son Peter.

The "church has been her life" does not end with Bessie's physical death. Last week in morning prayers here, I was talking about a heavy theological word, 'Eschatology'. 'Eschatology' tries to get across the idea that what is eternal begins in the here and now. The church life that we enjoy here is part of the Church Triumphant that exists already in heaven. The teaching of the New Testament is not that we go to God when we die, but that God has come to us in Jesus Christ whilst we are alive. We enter into eternal life through belief in Jesus Christ in the here and now while we are alive and not just when we die. Jesus in John 5:24 says, "Whoever hears my words and believes in Him who sent me has eternal life. He (let's make that she) will not be judged, but has already passed from death to life." In the Here and Now-not in the, There and Then!

Anyone believing in God may have the Old Testament hope of life after death, that there may be something beyond this life.

Anyone believing in Jesus Christ has the New Testament assurance that we have "already passed from death to life".

That's why the New Testament talks about death as "Falling asleep in Christ" That's a lovely image with which to think about death. Yes, "The Church has been her whole life." And it continues to be her whole life in death. We simply thank God for her life and witness as we sing the hymn 196

> **I know that my Redeemer lives-**
> **What joy the blest assurance gives!**
> **He lives, he lives who once was dead;**
> **He lives, my everlasting Head.**

NEEDHAM: Norman died 2nd March 1994 aged 76

Just over five years ago we had the funeral service here for Norman Needham's wife, Bessie. In that service we picked up on something that Norman had said about her in conversation, "The church has been her whole life." The same might be said of Norman, but his involvement in church was different. Norman was by training and by nature an intensely practical man.

Norman had the traditional up-bringing in the church of 70 years ago which was augmented by attending Norbury Church Day School. That early training and background led to a commitment to Jesus Christ and his church for life. A commitment that survived the hurly burly of being an apprentice joiner in the rough and ready world of the building trade with Marslands. A commitment that carried him through the years of the second world war as he served as a bombardier in Egypt and the Middle East. Like so many who served he talked little about it on his return but, unlike so many, what he experienced during war-time served to strengthen his faith.

Norman returned home to happier times, marrying Bessie at Napier Street Methodist Church on the 19/5/45 and their son Peter was born two years later in 1947. The year of the bad winter wasn't it-you were too young to remember Peter! Though the church was Norman's life just as much as Bessie's, he went out and about too. His enthusiasm for music had him playing piano for the Primary Department at Napier Street, playing Cornet in the Hazel Grove Brass Band, joining with the Norbury Players in performing Gilbert & Sullivan operas, and being a member of the choir in the churches to which he belonged.

Whether producing and performing plays with the Wesley Players, bowling with the Norbury Bowling Club, or latterly cavorting with the youngsters in Playgroup, Norman exhibited that same degree of commitment and enthusiasm that made him such stimulating company.

It was that, more than anything else that endeared him to his throng of ministering-usually female-angels who kept an eye on him after Bessie died and did more and more for him when he was practically housebound during the past two years.

To Peter, who so lovingly cared and prepared the flat at Birch House, to relatives and those friends, Norman would want me to say thank you.

When you think of all this, his apprenticeship as a carpenter, his later involvement with the building side of the NW Hospital Board at Stockport and before his retirement as a Clerk of Works for Cheshire County Council, it's not easy to remind ourselves that Norman suffered from emphysema for so many years. There were times when he could hardly draw breath, but he continued to live life to the full, apart from the latter years.

When I came to Bramhall someone described Norman to me as the Clerk of Works for the new Church Centre. He supervised the building of the Centre on behalf of the church and would have done the same with Centrepoint for us had he been well enough. Norman was a 'Clerk of Works' through and through from his greeting with raised arm, "How ya doing", through to his careful checking of the building side of the work for which he was responsible.

Like anyone who has a responsible job to do and does it properly, he could upset people with his steady determination to have the job done right, but everyone knew exactly "where Norman was coming from" in modern day parlance.

The work of a Godly Clerk of Works is described in the OT. That man's name was Nehemiah-Needham/Nehemiah-not that much difference! Nehemiah was a soldier and statesman who helped organise the rebuilding of the walls of Jerusalem after the Babylonian exile.

Alexander Whyte, the great Scottish preacher described Nehemiah as,

"A self-contained man. A man of his own counsel. A man with the counsel of God alone in his mind and in his heart. A reserved and resolute man. A man to take command of other men. He will not begin till he has counted the cost. And then he will not stop till he has finished the work."

That will do as an epitaph for Norman Needham.

He counted the cost of commitment to Jesus Christ in his early years, and despite being saddened by the loss of his beloved Bessie and dogged by ill-health in his later years, he did not stop until he had finished the work that God gave him to do.

We thank God for all that he has shared with us.

NICOL: Stanley I. R. died 22nd July 1992 aged 67

I have been promising myself for some years that I would get round to preaching on the three gardens of scripture, the Garden of Eden, the Garden of Gethsemane, and the Garden of the Resurrection. Those gardens came to my mind last Wednesday, the day that Stan Nicol died.

THE GARDEN OF EDEN symbolises those things in our lives that God has planned for us and which have given us great pleasure. To sum them up for Stan would be to include work, church and family. The family sometimes felt that Stan thought about them in that order too! **Work for Stan** in aeronautical engineering, for forty odd years, was also a hobby. He loved aeroplanes and the family reckon that there is hardly a family film to be found that does not drift from family up into the skies to pick out an aeroplane flying past. Stan was an enthusiast about planes and could name them as they flew overhead. He even knew the timetables by which many of them flew. A fortunate man to be able to derive so much pleasure from his work.

Church for Stan was a second career. He brought to it the same whole-hearted commitment that motivated him at work. Stan could never be casual about his commitment to Jesus Christ and the church. Since he came to Bramhall in 1946, I think it is true to say that every aspect of this church's life has been enhanced by Stan's dedicated service. Talk of young people and Stan's name will be mentioned in all age groups from Sunday School to the Youth Club. Practically, he did a stint on most church committees and pastorally his gifts were used in everything from class leadership to becoming Senior Church steward in 1974. Christian Aid, Methodist Homes for the Aged, Probus, Communicare and countless other caring services of the church benefitted from this willing servant but I think I, and possibly the family, treasure most the comment that has come from so many individuals who have joined this church in the past 46 years,

"Stan was the first person to welcome me."

Our families know us best of all, and it is a tribute to the kind of family relationships Stan and Anne have nurtured during their long and happy years of married life that they can be so open and honest about each other. Like many from north of the border, Stan did not find it easy to express his deep love for his family in words, but he demonstrated it by his actions. He was ever available for those desperate emergencies that always seem to affect young people in their teenage years. Many are the stories that could be told, but it's his children, Alison, Sheena and Iain who hold the copyright. Stan had a gift for friendship. His quiet friendliness and sense of humour conquered the language barrier and won the hearts of a second family in Spain, where they had a service for Stan earlier this week. **None of the family would want Stan portrayed as a paragon of virtue.** Such dedication in work and church life carries with it the ever-present danger of a dogmatism about what is right and what is wrong that is not easy to cope with-especially when teenagers are growing up and they have their own dogmatic views on life. The great redeeming feature in Stan was that his certainties were always tempered with such a love for his family and other people that strained relationships were not allowed to last. He could be almost pedantic about the use of grammar and fastidious in his desire to have, "a place for everything and everything in its place" but he learned to laugh at his own insistence that things should be done right. Family and friends loved him for that. But that was all IN THE GARDEN OF EDEN.

THE GARDEN OF GETHSEMANE became a reality over the past twelve months. For some time, the possibility had been there as tests and treatment failed to clear up the problems. Earlier this year we were told that Stan Nicol had only days to live. Countless people prayed, Stan and the medical profession fought and Stan was shared with us for another few months. It was at that time that Stan like his master before him set his face toward Jerusalem. He knew what was to come. None of us can imagine the spiritual as well as physical resources needed to fight his way back to church, to come to terms with his strong belief in the healing power of prayer and to face up to the death sentence that had been passed on him. Gethsemane is a lonely place and even those who loved him most were as the sleeping disciples as the battle was being fought. **At what point Stan was able to come to, "Not my will, however, but your will be done." we do not know,** all I do know is there came that point in time when Stan was able to share openly and to strengthen others by his own faith. No one who spent time with Stan over the past few weeks could have doubted his assurance and his peace in Christ. Many who went to minister in friendship found themselves ministered to by Stan's wry smile and strong faith.

THE GARDEN OF RESURRECTION cannot be fully experienced by those who have not enjoyed Eden or endured Gethsemane. Acknowledgement of God's care of us in the Garden of Eden prepares us for the time of suffering and seeming separation in the Garden of Gethsemane. The Resurrection that follows comes like the glorious bursting forth of spring flowers after a harsh winter. It seemed sad to many of us at first that at the time when Stan died, Anne had popped out for a few minutes to sit in the garden at the centre of Christie Hospital. Outside the hospital is the main road with the noise of passing traffic. Around the garden are the wards which have seen such suffering, sadness and pain, but as we came back down from Stan's bedside that sheltered garden haven at the very centre of so much turmoil was bathed in sunshine. We were being reminded of the Resurrection. The garden of Resurrection is bathed in the sunshine of God's love and like the rainbow in the storm says to all who will listen, God cares for you. "Let not your hearts be troubled, neither let them be afraid."

THE THREE GARDENS: EDEN; GETHSEMANE; RESURRECTION symbolise our faith. Don't look for their location in a place, but in the faith that Stan had, that the God who gave us Eden, is with us in Gethsemane, and will continue to bless us in the Garden of Resurrection. **Our Christian faith celebrates the fact that God walks with us in the Garden of Eden, suffers with us in Gethsemane, and raises faithful servants like Stan Nicol to new life in the Resurrection. Thanks be to God.**

OVERALL: Sidney died 5th May 1993 aged 92

I NEVER KNEW SIDNEY OVERALL AS A LONDON BLACK CAB TAXI DRIVER but, from all accounts, he was a good one. Could there have been a more suitable job for a Cockney lad born within the sound of Bow Bells? Somehow this sense of rightness is the underlying theme in the harmony that runs through the life that Sid led for 90 odd years. I suppose that his small stature would have fitted him for the life of a Newmarket jockey, which was in his father's thinking. Having been to Grammar School, he might have made a go of being the city gent with a firm of publishers where he began work. You can even see him hard at work in his father's thriving "Harry Ramsden" of coffee stalls serving the theatre and other night life of London where he worked for a while. 100lbs of sausages! But by 1921 Sid had made up his mind about the job that was to keep him happy for the rest of his life. It took him a couple of years, even as a London lad born and bred to cycle and walk round the streets of London learning names of roads, important places, and the most direct routes before he could present himself to the Home Office for examination. He cabbied for almost 60 years in London without an accident and his job gave him a lifetime of memories that continued to keep him happy in retirement at 79 years of age. **He ferried the famous like the late queen, Mary, and the Prince of Wales.** Show people like Googie Withers were recalled with fondness and dangerous or humorous situations could be brought to mind as though they happened yesterday. Sid laughed at the thinking of a Jewish client who specifically asked for a Christian cab driver rather than a Jewish one because he would have no conscience in complaining if he was overcharged by a Christian! Sid enjoyed a laugh and earned the nickname of smiler among his fellow drivers. His sense of humour stood him in good stead in the London days of the blitz when grown men cried at what they discovered as they shared in rescue work. Nevertheless, Sid would tell you that he had a lot to smile about. He loved his work as a cab driver. He had a happy marriage with his first wife Cissie, in Sidcup, Kent. He was blessed with a lovely daughter Pat. Sadness followed in the death of his beloved wife.

After 18 years as a widower, during which Sid travelled widely, romance entered his life once gain. He was a regular visitor to a hotel in Swanage where he and, as it turned out, his wife-to-be, Flo, enjoyed dancing. They married in 1974 and Sid set out on a new adventure by coming to live in the north for the first time. He loved the place and the people. In 1989 he was delighted to be able to give full expression to his deep Christian faith and make a response to the warm fellowship that he found in this church by joining his much-loved Flo in becoming a member here at the age of 87. Even at that age, he joined the Tuesday Fellowship and Thursday Bible Study until the time when old age and ill health curtailed his attendance in church. It was especially then and when, sadly, his daughter Pat died a little while ago that Sid and Flo appreciated the visits and loving care offered by ordinary members of this church. It would be inappropriate to single out individuals for mention, but I well remember Sid recounting in detail the special trip that one couple had given them to see the Christmas lights in Manchester. Sid's love of life shone through and his appreciation and thankfulness to all those of you who helped him continue to enjoy it knew no bounds.

Like a well-known character, Zacchaeus in the bible, Sid would have had to climb a tree to see Jesus in a crowd. Somewhere in his busy life as a London cab driver Sid looked out over the crowds and saw Jesus. All that he did was an expression of the love and peace that God had given him. There was no Jesus sticker in his cab but, his love of life and his work; his sense of humour and his smiling face; his understanding of God's word and his commitment to prayer; were their own witness to everyone with whom he came into contact. How many thousands would that be in a working life spanning almost 60 years? As with Zacchaeus, Jesus saw Sid long before Sid acknowledged Jesus, but in the end it all fitted together. It was so right!

We are just thankful that in these last few years Sid invited Jesus into his own heart and home, that he found his Christian home with us in this church for a while, and that he is now at home with Jesus Christ.

OWEN: Frank died 20th June 1996 aged 93

The family chose the hymn "Lord of all hopefulness" for the service this morning. The author Jan Strother is well known for her novel "Mrs. Miniver "which won seven Oscars as a film starring Greer Garson and Walter Pidgeon. You'll remember it well Theresa. The hymn is helpfully set out in four verses symbolising morning, noon, evening and night in any day, but it also provides a focus for us in thinking about Frank Owen's life.

IN THE MORNING OF FRANK OWEN'S LIFE, he was blessed in his background and upbringing.

Frank Owen was born in Stockport in 1902 and his sister Dorothy was born two years later. At about the same time Frank was enrolled into the Cyclists Touring Club. His father was the Company Secretary at Sutton & Torkinton, one of the many hatting firms upon which the trade of Stockport was founded. He attended Brentnall Street School, which is now the Masonic Lodge situated on the A6, until 1914 when he was awarded one of the two scholarships available to attend Stockport Grammar School.

From being a very small baby he was taken on holiday, usually to Friog near Barmouth in Wales, as a member of a large family group, and in recent years he enjoyed holidays in Aberdovey, where he would relive the times spent in that area in the early years of this century.

IN THE AFTERNOON OF FRANK OWEN'S LIFE activity was the name of the game.

Frank started his working career in the Bramhall branch of the Lancashire and Yorkshire Bank, later to become Martins Bank and then Barclays, in the building now occupied by the Royal Bank of Scotland. Banking was very different in those days as he told of the times when people used to ride up to the door of the bank and the staff would have to take the money out to them.

From Bramhall he moved to the Manchester branch in Great King Street. Whilst there during the war he had to do spells of fire watching duty during the night. This was followed by a period at Stockport and he finished his career in charge of the branch at New Mills.

Frank's great love, after his wife Theresa, was cycling and he went everywhere by bicycle, even cycling to work in New Mills every day until he retired. He even took a longer way home some evenings just for the fun of it. He cycled pretty well every road in England, Wales and Scotland and he would take you down numerous country lanes to avoid the traffic, a map was never needed. That early enrolment into the Cyclists Touring Club, meant membership was held for the rest of his life. From the time when he possessed his own bicycle his holidays were spent touring the length and breadth of the British mainland, either with his family, a friend from the bank or alone. On one of his lone tours, he ventured across to the Island of Mull and was given accommodation at a large family run farm called Ardnacross. There he met Theresa, for whom his nickname has always been "Treasure". That chance meeting led to their being married at an hotel in Callander, in September 1935. Sheila was their only daughter, but they gained a son when she married Ted in 1961.

IN THE EVENING OF FRANK OWEN'S LIFE, he was able to indulge his love of family life.

Fiery Frank, for he could be quite lively in temper, mellowed with age and was delighted when first Kathy, then Janet and Christine were born. He spent many happy hours in the early days of his retirement wheeling them out in their prams and he and Theresa enjoyed taking them for outings in the car. As his family was his greatest love and he liked "to have something to worry about" he spent last year wondering whether Janet would be safe as she travelled around the world and more recently whether Christine and Peter's baby would arrive safely. Happily, he was able to see Matthew Simon and was thrilled to become a Great Grandad.

THE NIGHT TIME CAME TO THE LIFE OF FRANK OWEN as it comes to all who live to a good age.

Memories and nostalgia take the place of the activities that once were. Frank, who enjoyed all aspects of family, traced his ancestry back to a distant relationship with Wilfred Owen, the first World War poet. Apart from his cycling he enjoyed gardening and stamp collecting and he was an extensive reader until the latter years when his sight began to fail. He was never happier than when he was visiting old haunts with Theresa and the family. He had no great desire to travel abroad. As he put it, "flying in an aeroplane was too far to jump and he never learnt to swim". He just appreciated the joys of the British countryside. Last year, family and friends were delighted to be able to join Frank and Theresa in the celebration of their Diamond Wedding.

THE HYMN HIGHLIGHTS THE Morning of hopefulness, the afternoon of eagerness, the evening of kindliness, so much the pattern of Frank Owen's life, but then what?

My memories of cycling days (touch of nostalgia there), of cycling fifteen miles to work each day and fifteen miles back remind me of how, when you were going downhill on a bike, the hill on the other side looked much steeper than it really was when you got on to it. **I think death is a little like that. Worse in the anticipation than in the reality.** The Bible talks about death as "Falling asleep in Christ". Falling asleep and waking up to a new morning where "He will wipe away all tears from their eyes. There will be no more death, no more grief or crying or pain." That's the "new heaven and new earth". (Rev 21) How does the hymn end?

Lord of all gentleness, Lord of all calm,
Whose voice is contentment, whose presence is balm,
Be there at our sleeping, and give us we pray,
Your peace in our hearts, Lord, at the end of the day.

That was Frank Owen's experience and is now a prayer for us all!

PARKER: Reginald died 30th July 1992 aged 66

"JESUS SAW NATHANAEL COMING TO HIM AND SAID OF HIM, "BEHOLD AN ISRAELITE INDEED, IN WHOM IS NO GUILE.'" JOHN 1:47

I understand that I am not alone in thinking that Reg Parker was a most unlikely Police Inspector, for he was a man without guile. Somehow, he served for thirty years in the police force without being tainted by the cynicism that sometimes affects those who have to cope with human behaviour at its worst.

You could picture him as the conscientious caring village policeman or even a musically-minded Inspector Morse located in a university town, but hardly an Inspector in the Manchester City Police.

Reg was such a gentle and sincere person that it is difficult to associate him with criminal investigations that depend so much on entering into the minds of those whose tendencies are totally different. Yet it was those self-same qualities that made him a good policeman.

Had you known him as a Bevan boy working in the pits of Doncaster or on the land after the war. If your association with Reg was from the time when he was tug of war champion for the R.A.F or when he was being presented to our present Queen then Princess Elizabeth while appearing in the Royal Tournament of 1948.

If you had come into contact with him as a policeman in Cheshire or an Inspector in Manchester. Whether you knew him as a Yorkshireman in the church who not only called a spade a spade, but was prepared to dig with it too, or as someone put it as "a gardener with arsonist tendencies." No matter what the setting Reg came across as a man without guile.

IN FAMILY LIFE I reckon being tug-of-war champion helped him cope perfectly with being married to the strong-minded and soft-hearted Jean for forty years. He was never happier than when she and the family were on one end of the rope and he on the other. Lovely stories of how this intensely practical man would cut through Jean and Elizabeth's teacher-like analysis of the bad behaviour of a school child by saying quite simply, "The child was having an off day." It was an attitude mellowed by age that made him the perfect grandfather.

Reg was a practical man around the home, but he was also a perfectionist. Every job had to be done right. That could take time and cause a certain amount of tension for others who would like to make do and mend. He was a typical Yorkshireman who could express very strong views about the waste associated with royalty and ceremonial occasions when there was so much need in the world, but untypical in that he could listen to others with different views.

Reg and Jean have travelled widely, but Reg was content to enjoy the simple pleasures of life. That's why the flowers today are simple bunches and not wreaths with all the trimmings. Just a week or two ago his son Mike asked if he wanted a drive out somewhere, anticipating a response of, perhaps Lyme Park. Reg said yes, he would very much like to take some bottles to the bottle bank. Reg was a true Yorkshireman, without guile, pretence or pretension, but there was more to the man that Reg became than that innate simplicity which people found so appealing.

THE INTEGRITY IN THE MAN SO EVIDENT THROUGHOUT HIS LIFE PROMPTED A SPIRITUAL PILGRIMAGE.
It was Philip who brought Nathanael to Jesus and Jesus awakened faith in Nathanael by saying, "Before Philip called you, when you were under the fig tree, I saw you." The gentle Christian influence of Jean and others, including Billy Graham, in early days bore fruit in the ministry of a Chaplain Hirst in Germany in the mid-fifties.

The commitment that Reg made at that time, was akin to that of Nathanael on his first meeting with Jesus, "Rabbi, you are the Son of God! You are the King of Israel!" Reg responded to his personal encounter with God with the same pragmatism that had stamped its mark on the whole of his life. There was no going back on that commitment to Christ and his Church. Regular church worship became a priority in life and the same discipline that he had undertaken in the R.A.F. and the police force was applied to his Christian discipleship.

The Bramhall Methodist church trip to the Holy Land coincided with his retirement from the police force in 1986. It was when Reg and Jean shared in that pilgrimage that Reg's faith became what John Wesley called, "a disposition of the heart" as well as a "train of ideas in the head". The Holy Land changed Reg dramatically and with hindsight we can know that the change prepared him for what was to come.

REG, NO MORE THAN NATHANAEL NEARLY TWO THOUSAND YEARS EARLIER, could have known what was to follow his commitment to Christ. Nathanael is not mentioned again in John's Gospel until the 21st chapter where he is named as one of those disciples who met with the Risen Lord Jesus Christ by the sea of Galilee. Reg Parker committed himself to the way of Jesus in Germany, but he found his deep assurance with the Risen Lord Jesus Christ near that same Sea of Galilee.

IT WAS STILL THE SAME REG WHO CAME BACK.
A man "in whom is no guile". The straightforward pragmatist who helped the family cope with the sadness's of recent years, but there was the added dimension of a deep faith that knew God's love and expressed it in word as well as in action. He showed that same calm in crisis that he had always shown when he knew that his illness was terminal, but that calm was enriched by a serenity and peace that testified to his faith in His Risen Lord. The end came mercifully quickly after Reg went into St. Ann's Hospice last Monday.

On Tuesday Elizabeth came. The children and the new baby George went to see grandfather at St. Ann's. The end came peacefully with the family on hand. **As Mike, so wisely, put it. "Another perfect job done, dad."**

"Another perfect job done "as our Father in heaven took the simple faith of this man without guile, reinforced it with the assurance of his love and made of Reg, a testimony to love's victory over suffering and death. Reg had come to know that death was only the end of the beginning of eternal life.

It's a faith so beautifully expressed in the hymns that Reg chose.

"Blessed Assurance, Jesus is mine, O what a foretaste of glory divine:"

"Dear Lord & Father of mankind, forgive our foolish ways", with the imagery of the Holy Land to the fore, and the triumphant,

"Thine be the glory, Risen Conquering Son,
endless is the victory thou oe'r death hast won."

Let's enter into the spirit of that Holy Land pilgrimage and find the assurance that Reg found as we sing,

**"In simple trust like theirs who heard
Beside the Syrian sea
The gracious calling of the Lord,
Let us like them, without a word
Rise up and follow thee."**

PARKES: W. May died 11th November 1989 aged 85

May Parkes had three great loves in her life, the church, her family and the scouts. It was a happy circumstance that allowed her to be surrounded by all three last Friday evening, the night before she passed peacefully away on the Saturday morning. May has given a lifetime's service to the church and with her late husband Bob was actively involved in the scouting movement from her early days. May was never happier than when she was actively involved in doing everything from tea-making to fund-raising as a backroom girl in the Oakwood Methodist Church to which she belonged in London. It was, perhaps, because she was so actively involved in the church there that she found it difficult to adjust to her new church home in Bramhall. Her move here coincided with the onset of old age for this youthful 80-year-old and ill-health began to restrict her activities causing her some unhappiness. She was impatient with the old age and ill-health that began to slow her down. May didn't want to be a burden to anyone and she didn't like having to depend upon other people. She herself admitted that she would have been an awful invalid to nurse. Set her talking about life in her old church and she came alive with the history and the excitement of it all.

May's interest in the Scouting movement never waned and she still thought it the finest of organisations for young people to be involved in. To see the youngsters and especially her own family in scout uniform was a great joy to her and David's position as scoutmaster made her very proud. She was always interested in what was happening in the world and like so many who have lived through a century of great change, she was saddened by what she saw as a decline in standards, particularly with the young. I'm sure that May saw the scouting movement as a defence against such a decline and would have had every youngster doing National Service in the scouts or guides if she had had her way! Even when her body began to let May down, her lively mind continued to express her concern for the larger world and she was thrilled at recent developments in East Germany and at any moves towards peaceful co-existence in her world that has seen so much of war. The love that motivated May Parkes was sometimes hidden by a frankness and honesty that could be disconcerting to the unprepared. They talk about blunt northerners; true Londoners take some beating. Her caring love was seen at its best in the devoted nursing care given to her late husband, Bob, over many years of ill health, but it was the same love that was shared with her son David, Sue and grandchildren Matthew & Naomi. May loved their times together and was glad to see them belonging in church and the scouting movement.

That was very important to May, to feel that you belonged to church, to scouts and in family life. For such an active person it is interesting to note that her favourite authors of devotional books were the very modern and meditative Frank Topping and the comfort filled writings of Helen Steiner Rice. These two writers symbolise May Parkes' faith. The thoughtful and challenging Frank Topping balanced by simplicity of Helen Steiner Rice.

May Parkes was very aware that she belonged above all to God. What needs to be said about death in the face of such assurance? There was no doubt for May who she belonged to in this life and who she was going to in the next. She loved and served Jesus in this life and expected to be with him in the next. Those of you who belong to this church will know that young Matthew produced our notice sheet cover a couple of weeks ago. It had an angel on the front with the caption Bramhall Methodist Church welcomes you. If they have a notice sheet in heaven, Matthew and Naomi, it will be saying the same thing to your gran. Heaven welcomes you.

Two weeks ago, in a sermon about death in this church I reminded the congregation of how the N.T. after the resurrection of Jesus talks about Christians who die as "falling asleep in Christ". **May Parkes actually fell asleep in her son David's arms and would wake up in the arms of God's Son Jesus. That is His promise which May believed and so can we.**
We sing the hymn-Blessed Assurance, Jesus is mine

ROBINSON: Harry H. died 18th May 1993 aged 71

What do you say about a man who has meant so much in so many different ways to countless people in the few minutes that we have available to us here? A minister of music, as organist, to everyone at times of significance in their family lives, baptisms, marriages and funerals and here in the regular worship of this church. Harry was as much called and dedicated to his ministry as any ordained minister. On reflection I decided that I couldn't do much more than evoke a few memories that will remind us of the debt that we owe to Harry Robinson as family, friends and members of the churches in which he has served.

MEMORIES OF THE PRIVATE BUT SELF-RELIANT MAN, PERHAPS KNOWN ONLY TO HIS FAMILY AND VERY CLOSE FRIENDS.

Harry was a designer draughtsman who worked for a variety of engineering companies in this area and North Wales. He was an interesting man because he was an interested man. Interested in what made everything tick from a car engine to the human body. It has been suggested that Harry was a do-it-yourself kind of person, but I think that would convey the wrong impression. Certainly, my kind of DIY which is a combination of brute force and ignorance and make do and mend would never have been Harry's way.

Harry's mind tackled any problem with the designer draughtsman's aptitude for reflecting before perfecting. We had no sooner thought of re-designing the former choir area than Harry had carefully worked out alternatives of how many chairs would fit into the space and how they might be positioned. Harry spent countless hours making everything from an early T.V. set to an electronic organ. If he couldn't buy the part that he wanted he would make it. Some of the very special sounds that he was able to produce on this organ were through Harry's own electronic innovations.

MEMORIES TOO OF THE QUIET, BASICALLY SHY, PERSON BECOME PUBLIC PERFORMER.

The dance band of younger years with piano, violin, drummer and accordion laid the foundation for the man who was to become almost unique as a church organist. His training and work as an organist combined with his interest in popular music to share with the church that special blend of traditional church music and the lighter mood engendered by popular songs which bore the stamp of Harry's own arrangement and versatility in presentation. I will not remember Harry for his organ recitals, and that will not surprise some of you who are aware of my lack of appreciation of classical music.

What memories come to mind with his first rendition of Sleigh Ride on this organ, sleigh bells and all on Christmas Day. The faces of the young children in the church were a picture as they listened. Whose wedding was it when it poured down and Harry broke into "Raindrops Fallin' on My Head"? So often there would be a look of puzzlement on the faces of the congregation as the incidental music was being played in worship and we said to ourselves, I know that tune-what is it?

There followed that smile of realization that Harry was harmonising his own arrangement of a popular song. Memories of the offering being taken in the church and the collectors finding themselves bouncing back down the aisle to the rhythm of "The Lonely Goatherd". In a more subdued and devotional vein we found ourselves listening to his own rendition of Simon and Garfunkel's "Bridge over Troubled Water" or "The Sound of Silence."

What might not always have been acknowledged in the seeming spontaneity is the fact that so much of what Harry shared with us was the outcome of countless hours of practice and meticulous preparation for every service in which he was involved.

MEMORIES TOO OF THE MUSIC THAT SO FITTED THE MOOD OF THE MOMENT.

Harry was a sensitive person who could be easily hurt. Not for him the histrionics which tend to be labelled artistic temperament, but like most of us who are up-front in these situations he could be upset by criticism or even because he himself felt that he had not done as well as he might have done. That sensitivity was his greatest gift. He was able to tune into the mood of the moment and somehow feel rather than think his way to what was right for any circumstance. Perhaps the greatest danger for the isolated organist is that he can become distant from people. People always came first with Harry. He was a musician with the heart of a pastor. A largely non-church-going family were thrilled to hear the theme music for their mother's favourite programme being gently played as they left this church after her funeral service. For them Harry proved that the church cared.

His sensitivity was a gift, but like most gifts it owed much to the Giver. In Harry's case there was never any question as to who the Giver was. Harry was able to tune into the mood of the moment because he was in tune with God. It was my privilege as a minister like others before me to hear Harry, not only playing the organ, but also praying with me. Just occasionally, Harry would enter so deeply into worship himself that there was a pause before his sharing with God gave way once again to his leading of worship.

MEMORIES OF THE MAN AND HIS MUSIC, BUT MEMORIES TOO OF A MAN OF DEEP FAITH.

Harry was devoted to Jesus Christ, his church and his family, usually in that order. Edna and the family knew the warmth of his love for them and their devotion to each other was self-evident. Their home has been a place of harmony and Christian love. There hurts were healed and Harry's ministry of music was renewed in the loving and very practical support that Edna has offered.

Every person with whom Harry came into contact became aware of his sensitivity and concern for them. All of us in this church have been blessed by the man as well as his music. I, like many others, have been privileged to feel the touch of Christ upon my life through the ministry that Harry Robinson has shared with us. Jesus at the very heart of that Communion service so loved by Harry said, "This do in Remembrance of Me". There is little that any of us will do in the worship life of this church that will not evoke memories of Harry. We shall cope best with his death when we remember with thankfulness and realise that as with death of Jesus, the memories, the man and his music, live on. Thanks be to God.

INDEPENDENTLY OF MY PREPARATION HARRY'S SON, JOHN, HAD PUT TOGETHER A BRIEF MEDLEY OF THREE SONGS THAT HARRY USED TO PLAY IN REVERSE ORDER.

Bridge Over Troubled Water-
When tears are in your eyes, I'll dry them all.

Moonlight and Roses-
And wonderful memories of you.

and Nana Maskouri's,
Try to remember the kind of September when life was slow and oh so mellow.

Deep in December it's nice to remember, and if you remember, Harry's **Follow, Follow, Follow, I will follow Jesus**

Our memories of Harry will become more meaningful as we follow the example he has given us in Jesus Christ, of gracious living and sacrificial service.

ROTHWELL: Alma died 27th December 1995 aged 87

To pop singing enthusiasts of my generation, the name Alma will always be linked with **Alma Cogan: "the girl with a laugh in her voice." Alma Rothwell, was for me: "The lady with the laugh in her eyes." It was that "laughter in her eyes"**, welling up from her heart that redeemed the sometimes forbidding exterior of the person whose life we remember here today. Perhaps, I move on too quickly!

Alma was born on the 16th May 1908, the fifth child in a family of six children. It was a very different world then! A few days before Alma was born, the government of the day had announced plans to introduce an Old Age Pension that would be worth 5 shillings per week to every single person over 70 and the princely sum of seven and sixpence to each married couple. With a life expectancy of three score years and ten at the time, the government were not planning to go bankrupt in the process. Alma might have been counting on collecting a civil service pension when she trained as a telephone operator, but she only lasted in that occupation until she was twenty-four.

After seven years of courtship, a new career lay before Alma in 1932. She married her late husband George, and they moved to a new bungalow in Gatley where Pauline was born. The family moved to Southport in 1938 and Anne arrived in 1942. It wasn't the shock of the new arrival that nearly killed Alma, but pneumonia. Alma survived and was able to say that she would never again be afraid of dying because she had felt so calm and peaceful at that time. How much that peace and calm was associated with her faith in God then, it is difficult to know. What was very clear throughout Alma's life was that she had been grounded in a religious faith that was typical of so much of church teaching in the early part of this century.

Her background was Anglican and she was proud of the fact that she had been confirmed by one who many would see as the greatest Anglican Archbishop of this century, William Temple. Her inflexible attitude toward many social problems and to the evils of drink in particular made her a solid companion to her dyed in the wool Methodist husband, George. Her strong views could so easily have deteriorated into self-righteousness, had it not been for the fact that she was even harder on herself than on other people.

Alma's beloved William Temple once said:

"Love of God is the root, love of our neighbour the fruit of the Tree of Life. Neither can exist without the other, but the one is cause and the other effect." Alma loved God and her relationships with other people were a fruit of her own relationship with God. Her friendships were sustained from a distance by good old fashioned letter writing.

American contacts included the mother of Anne's pen friend and a former GI whom she met in Southport. More unlikely was George and Alma's befriending of a former German prisoner of war who came into the post office at Southport to post a letter home and became the beneficiary of practical help until the Berlin Wall came down. Personal correspondence continued with Rolf, the East Gennan, and Yakub a Pakistani soldier and member of their athletics team who would always visit on his return. Interesting how little we know about most people when they are alive!!!

Alma made many friends, but her greatest love and loyalty was reserved for her own family. Her strict attitude to life was never far from her thinking about bringing up a family in the right way and it doesn't seem to have done them too much harm! Letters returned by grandma to grandchildren were not a sign of her displeasure, but an opportunity for them to review the corrections that she had made to their grammar and spelling!

It was her family and her piano that would bring out the best in Alma. The laughter in her eyes was rarely hidden for long as she entertained.

I suppose George learned to live with it, having spent his wedding night helping his new bride to recover from too long spent on the piano at the wedding reception. She played for other people's pleasure, as well as her own. There can be no doubting Alma's love for God, for her family and her friends. I want to suggest that it is only in more recent years that Alma began more fully to appreciate God's love for her and how much she meant to so many people. God became very close to her as she struggled to cope with the loss of her husband George in 1988.

Worship became even more important to her and she came into membership of this church in 1989. Ill health dogged her last years, but she valued the pastoral caring of Maurice Wendt, Sheila Bothamley and their fellowship group. So much had she given, she found receiving hard. She told us several times that she was ready to go to God.

The laughter was still there when we implied that God might not be quite ready for her and was taking time to make sure that the place was properly sorted out for her arrival!! The last few years have seen a growth in grace to match her undoubted faith. I have the impression that duets go down rather better than solos in heaven!

I can't think that if Alma had any voice in these proceedings, she would refrain from giving one last piece of good advice to the next generation. It would be along the lines of the Philippians reading chosen by the family.

"In conclusion, my brothers, fill your minds with those things that are good and deserve praise: things that are noble, true, right, pure lovely and honourable. Put into practice what you learnt and received from me, both from my words and from my actions. And the God who gives us peace will be with you."

Phil 4.8-9.

ROTHWELL: Arthur died 28th March 1993 aged 79

A friend writing to express sympathy to the Rothwell family suggested that the words of Micah 6.8 might have been written for Arthur Rothwell. **"WHAT DOTH THE LORD REQUIRE OF THEE, BUT TO DO JUSTLY, AND TO LOVE MERCY, AND TO WALK HUMBLY WITH THY GOD."**

Arthur's life was governed by what he understood the Lord required of him. TO DO JUSTLY OR TO DO WHAT IS RIGHT Doing what was right in his working life took him from being an office boy in Manchester Town Hall at 14 through night school and a University degree to being an accountant in the City Treasurer's Department where his career spanned forty good years.

That same sense of justice drove him to take an active part in Union affairs with NALGO, looking after the needs of his colleagues in a practical way. Arthur was ever the doer despite the serious illness in 1959 which left him weakened in body if not in spirit.

Obviously, his sense of what was right was stimulated and sustained by his Christian faith and in many ways, he typified the faithful and devoted Methodist of his generation. A lifelong teetotaller, he had no time for the other kind of spirit's way of generating good humour. Arthur's unfailing good humour was resourced at a much deeper level and communicated in private conversation and on public platform. A Methodist local preacher since 1935 and a Circuit Trainer of new Local Preachers, he had a real presence in the pulpit as his sense of what was right reinforced his message.

Less typically Methodist was his pacifist position in times when pacifism was not a popular cause to espouse. Arthur stood for what was right as he understood it, no matter how unpopular the cause.

His strong convictions rarely stifled his graciousness in the "fellowship of controversy", but there were times when he would be a little too certain for some of the rightness of his cause. More than once Arthur and I (and I suspect other people too) had to agree to disagree. Arthur and Louie made me very welcome when we came to this church some years ago, but my first really vivid memory of him is when I came out of the pulpit having preached a sermon that only lasted 15 minutes to find him shaking his head at the door with the comment, "Short measure this morning, wasn't it!" At the same time, Arthur was generous in praise of those leading worship whether organists or preachers. The praise was valued the more because people knew that when Arthur said something he meant it.

LOVE MERCY OR AS THE GOOD NEWS BIBLE PUTS IT, "SHOW CONSTANT LOVE".

It was that quality of love for people that shone through. and ameliorated any traits of what we tend to call stubbornness in other people and determination in ourselves. It was that constant love that invested his work. as a Sunday School teacher and Youth Leader at Wesley Road Methodist Church, Swinton, with a special quality well remembered by the many young people who were influenced by his words, prayers and example. It was that constant love that has been a feature of this family's life. Almost 55 years of marriage to Louie, the perfect partner for Arthur. She has been the softener added to the washing powder. Bringing up a family in the Christian faith, and having that love returned by the many friends made both inside the church and wherever Arthur has touched the lives of other people.

WALK HUMBLY WITH YOUR GOD

Arthur served God through the church as a Local Preacher, Circuit Steward, Society Steward and in countless other capacities in church life.

At one time he had thought of going into the ordained ministry of the Methodist Church, but he discerned his call and lived out his life as a layman in his beloved Methodist Church.

It is fitting that God has honoured his faithfulness by calling his son Malcolm into the ordained ministry. Arthur achieved much in his lifetime, even in the latter years when he was plagued by ill-health. There is much of which he had every right to be proud. There were few signs of pride in himself, proud of his wife-yes, of his family-yes, of the church to which he belonged and of the God whom he worshipped-yes, but Arthur himself simply lived out the text, "to do justly, and to love mercy, and to walk humbly with. thy God."

He's up there even now as the Methodist Local Preacher crying out,

"That's enough of me, what about the appeal to those who are here."

The text began with the question, "What doth the Lord require of thee?" I think Arthur would want me to leave that question with you today. "What doth the Lord require of thee?"

Today is April Fool's Day. Peter Fleming, one of a group of missionaries who died in the forests of Ecuador at the hands of the Auca Indians once said,

"He is no fool who gives what he cannot keep, to gain what he cannot lose."

Arthur Rothwell was no fool. The Cross of Christ on Good Friday leads us through to the glorious Resurrection of Easter Day.
Arthur Rothwell died in Christ.
He now lives with Christ in the presence of God.
Thanks be to God.

ROTHWELL: George died 12th February 1988 aged 80

The family chose for the second hymn 688, "Who would true valour see, let him come hither;" which seems very appropriate because George as a Methodist liked a good sing, but also because it is based on a poem about "Mr Valiant for Truth" from John Bunyan's Pilgrim's Progress. The three verses of the hymn speak of: Constancy; Courage; and Confidence, all of which have been illustrated in the life of George Rothwell.

1. CONSTANCY In the first verse we are invited to admire the constancy of Mr Valiant for Truth. George Rothwell began his pilgrim's progress with a Methodist background many years ago. Having set out as a Methodist, there was for George no looking back. His great love was for the Methodist Church and he belonged to it wherever he happened to be at that time in his life. He served the Methodist Church in whatever way was asked of him from the ordinary tasks required in every church right through to the key post of Society Steward. George wasn't like so many fair-weather Christians, looking at the weather or looking at the preacher for the day before deciding whether or not to go to worship. Even in his later years, when some grow weary of church attendance, George wanted to be in his pew here on Sunday mornings. Like Mr Valiant for Truth and many other Christians, George Rothwell had to find his way through the: 'Slough of Despond'; the 'Hill Difficulty'; the 'Valley of the Shadow of Death'; and 'Doubting Castle'; but if asked, I think that he would have responded with Bunyan's Pilgrim to: "Did none of these things discourage you?" "No, because, I still believed what Mr Tell-true had said and that carried me beyond them all." As Great-heart then said, "Then this was your victory, even your faith." Constancy of faith and consistency marked George's faith-life.

2. COURAGE There is no shortage, even today, of those who: "beset us round with dismal stories", and if George seemed a little intolerant at times, it was because, like his beloved Alma, he felt strongly about his convictions. The Constancy that was his strength could be his Achilles heel as this product of the early 1900's coped with standards and morality of the latter part of the 20th Century.

Certainly, George had the courage of his convictions and was never afraid to air them. But he displayed many other kinds of courage during the war years and in starting afresh with Southam sub post office in 1946. George Rothwell loved his work and loved to work. He couldn't bear to be idle, as his many jobs taken on after his so-called retirement showed. He displayed courage in fighting back after earlier illness and demonstrated that special kind of courage that is needed by those who are consciously facing up to their impending death. He was a grateful person, thankful for every kindness shown to him by doctors, nurses, carers, family and friends during these final few weeks. A gentleman in life, he maintained that dignity through to his death.

3. CONFIDENCE "Hobgoblin nor foul fiend Can daunt his spirit; He knows he at the end Shall life inherit." Certainly, true of George Rothwell. He was not that kind of man to succumb to fears that have no foundation in fact, that could not destroy his faith in Jesus Christ. George Rothwell's confident faith has influenced the lives of so many, not least those of his family, who knew him best, Alma, daughters Pauline, Anne and his grandchildren. Any person, Valiant for Truth, can be difficult to live with at times. I always reckon that John Wesley, like most dead saints, must be easier to live with in our memories than when he was alive. Wesley must have been very difficult to live with, because he was so sure in ministry that he was right! It is God's love working in and through such people that saves us and them from self-righteousness. George Rothwell would be the last person to see himself as a ready-made saint but, "Who would true valour see, let him come hither" and acknowledge a true pilgrim in George of Constancy, Courage and Confidence in the faith found as a youngster, through the Methodist Church. That faith he trusted in life continues with him death.

As we began with John Bunyan and Mr Valiant for Truth, so we end. "When the day that he must go hence was come, many accompanied him to the riverside, into which as he went, he said, 'Death where is thy sting?' And as he went down deeper, he said, 'Grave, where is thy victory?' So, he passed over and all the trumpets sounded for him on the other side." **Amen!**

SCURR: Frank died 8th September 1994 aged 79

Frank Scurr was the genuine article. What you saw with Frank was what you got. A big and sometimes blunt engineer who displayed a gentleness of touch in relation to others that belied the outward appearance. But then I am jumping ahead of myself. Our next hymn, upon which I want to focus our thoughts about God and about Frank, in that order, was chosen for us by our organist Sylvia Reindel.

Hymn 42 to which you may like to turn begins:
**O LOVE OF GOD, HOW STRONG, HOW TRUE,
ETERNAL AND YET EVER NEW;**

A reminder that because God's love is so strong, it will never let us go and because it is so true, it will never let us down. Frank Scurr was one of the first group of people that I brought into membership here on the 3/7/1988. He had a firm faith in a loving God that had been nurtured in the Roman Catholic Church, but he had come to love the hymns and fellowship of the Free Church tradition. I'm not sure whether it was the Roman Catholic influence that caused him to marry three Marys in succession, but certainly each one of those Marys had a great influence on his life in different ways. That love of God so strong and true was the inspiration for the life of Frank Scurr.
**O HEAVENLY LOVE, HOW PRECIOUS STILL,
IN DAYS OF WEARINESS AND ILL.**

Weariness may be due to many things: infirmity, old age, loneliness, sorrow or depression. It was when other people were feeling these things that Frank's gruff cheerfulness came into its own. Frank knew what it was to "lose a loved one" and while coping with the handicap experienced by his second wife Mary, Frank's caring nature came into its own. Many in the Friday club had good reason to thank God for Frank's physical strength and his gentleness as he man-handled wheelchairs, but was so sensitive to their personal needs.

It was to Frank they turned at St. Michael's or for manning the lift that got them safely to and from their rooms on club holidays. Frank was a willing chauffeur for most of the organisations in this church at one time or another. I well remember this big man's gentle kindness as he helped little Mabel Brown get into church every Sunday morning. During the last couple of years Frank and Mary were to know many a night of pain and helplessness. Frank's practical and caring ministry had already relieved that sense of helplessness for many strugglers down the years.

**O WIDE EMBRACING WONDROUS LOVE,
WE READ THEE IN THE SKY ABOVE:**

& the following verse

**WE READ THEE BEST IN HIM WHO CAME
TO BEAR FOR US THE CROSS OF SHAME**

Life for Frank was the truest expression of God's love. He enjoyed it and never more than in these last few years as he and his beloved Mary lived out what would have been simply fantasy for Frank in the first world war years into which he was born. I only came to know this Mary when she and Frank were prepared for marriage in this church on the 17/9/88.

They had been good friends through Frank's second wife for years, so I think Frank knew what he was getting!!! He took Mary from work at many years past retiring age, married her, and brought her to Bramhall to share a wonderful few years together.

A good start was made when they went together on honeymoon to the hotel in Llandudno where they had gone regularly as separate individuals. They drew some old-fashioned looks at being willing to share a room together until they explained that they were now married. Christmases in Llandudno and holidays in Disney World were enjoyed alike because Mary and Frank were sharing them together.

Archbishop Temple insisted that the heart of the Christian gospel is not "God is love" but that "God so loved the world that he gave."

Frank & Mary gave much love to each other, but they shared it too with all whom they met in what turned out to be the twilight period of Frank's life. Mary's loss is summed up in her own semi-humorous words, "He brought me here to Bramhall but now he has left me!"

Even that sentiment is responded to in this hymn.

> **WE READ THY POWER TO BLESS AND SAVE**
> **E'EN IN THE DARKNESS OF THE GRAVE:**
> **STILL MORE IN RESURRECTION LIGHT**
> **WE READ THE FULLNESS OF THY MIGHT.**

That's the Christian teaching of the scriptures. On visiting in hospital Frank would say to me after our prayer together, "Prayer helps".

Frank's experience and ours is summed up in the final verse which is also a prayer. Mary, this is God's promise to you and a prayer for Frank.

> **O LOVE OF GOD, OUR SHIELD AND STAY**
> **THROUGH ALL THE PERILS OF OUR WAY;**
> **ETERNAL LOVE, IN THEE WE REST,**
> **FOR EVER SAFE, FOR EVER BLEST!**

SIMPSON: Mary died 3rd May 1994 aged 71

A Pieta is a representation, often in sculpture, of the mother of Jesus, Mary, lamenting over the dead body of Christ, which she holds on her knees. There is no scriptural authority for such a scene, but the emotive imagery has attracted artists down the years. Without doubt the most famous Pieta is that done by Michelangelo which can be viewed today in St. Peter's in Rome. In his Pieta, Michelangelo, idealises Mary's image by giving her a graceful young face and he gives the whole work of art its focus in the loving expression of Mary over the passive body of Jesus.

Mary Simpson was well named for she lived a life full of love and was loved much in return. Mary died within a quarter of a mile of where she was born and brought up in Poynton as Mary Wainwright, but she travelled a long way in her 71 years.

After Primary school in Poynton, she went to the Manchester Warehouseman and Clerks' School in Cheadle Hulme before starting work at the Liverpool and London and Globe Insurance Company in Albert Square, Manchester. Mary volunteered for the armed forces during the war, but was kept back in her reserved occupation.

That became a pattern for her life because Mary was never a front-line person. Her response was typical because she threw herself into voluntary work of various kinds. She joined the St. John's Ambulance Brigade and worked in the force's canteen in Poynton catering for the R.A.F. and U.S. Army forces.

Fortunately for Ron, Mary did not become a G.I. bride. Not only her occupation, but also her future husband was reserved for her when they met in the same insurance company after the war. Mary and Ron married in 1951 at the Park Lane Methodist Church in Hockley which Mary had attended since childhood.

The Methodist Church was Mary's life, but not her whole life. Her faith helped her to enjoy life in all its fullness and sent her out to be in contact with many people outside the church. Nevertheless, it was clear to everyone that it was her faith that determined the kind of person that she became. Her faith in God and commitment to Jesus Christ moved her to worship, fellowship and service in the life of the church. I, and I have no doubt, other ministers and preachers too, was encouraged by that quiet smile of contentment on the face of one who always seemed to be so composed. That composure didn't stop Mary geeing Ron up so that they wouldn't be on the last minute for sharing in what turned out to be her final communion service here in this church on Sunday, May 8th.

It was that same composure about the things that really mattered that freed Mary to be active in so many other ways. Church activities included Link and Christian Viewpoint for women, linking fellowship within with witness to those outside the church. Her calm composure made her an ideal carer whether over coffee here in the crush hall, in the Centrepoint Coffee Bar or the Thrift Shop. She would have become a Church Steward but she could not see herself standing there in an up-front role. She would have made a good one because as those who have shared in working with her testify, she cared about people and the witness to the love and peace she had found in her life showed.

The Evening Townswomen's Guild, Tennis Club, Local History Society at Poynton, the National Trust and above all Bridge Clubs at Marple and Woodford were blessed by the presence of this lovely lady who enjoyed life to the full and helped others enjoy it too.

She wasn't a gardener, but loved gardens.

She wasn't a photographer, as her family readily testify, but could enthuse over photographs.

She wasn't a political person in the real sense of the word, but became animated by "Question Time" on T.V.

Mary loved to travel whether to Scotland or New Zealand and she allowed every fresh experience to touch her heart as well as her mind. She wasn't a, "When I was in Singapore...." kind of person, but what she learned of Singapore gave her a more balanced reaction to the kind of justice that cleaned up that country than the semi-hysterical comments heard through the media in recent days. Mary by name and by nature focussed her love on foreigner, friend and family alike, but above all on her family.

Ron; Helen & Colin with children David & Nicola; John & Lynn with their new born twins, Bethany and Hannah due to be baptised in this church next month. All have known what it is to be loved in personal and practical ways by a wife, mother and grandmother who knew above all that she was loved by God. The stories are theirs to remember and to tell of family holidays and shopping trips, of care for relatives and neighbours, and especially for her grand-children that demonstrated a love for others that was stronger than her concern for herself. Her last words to Ron as she left home for her game of bridge last Tuesday evening were, "Now you have a rest." Mary has gone to her well-earned rest.

There may be no scriptural justification for the scene depicted in the Pieta of such love being expressed in the young face of Mary, but there is a great deal of scriptural warrant for the kind of love that found expression in the life of Mary Simpson.

That love was rooted in her faith, transformed her face and found expression in all that she did.

Here in Bramhall Methodist Church, we simply thank God for her life of love and know that her Lord now looks upon her with love in her death.

SLADE: Dora died 16th January 1993 aged 75

Much could be said about Dora Slade that would be news to many people gathered here. She was a private person who did not talk a great deal about herself and her background. Born in 1917 in Scotland, she became a Civil Servant as a teenager and moved to England. London became her home and she explored it in the only way that London can be properly explored, on foot. She was transferred to Portsmouth during the war and worked in the Admiralty there through the blitz.

It was during the war that she met another Civil Servant Jim, and they were married when transferred to Scotland in 1943. Michael was born a couple of years later. After a time in Hong Kong, the family lived in a variety of places in this country. There's a cover-all phrase that I remember from my days in the Civil Service used to justify whatever it wanted to do with people. "According to the Exigencies of the Service." The family were moved around in this country according to "the exigencies of the service", but in each place Dora was able to put down roots and make lasting friendships. The letters and cards of condolence from different parts of the country bear eloquent testimony to the love that she shared with so many. As has been said so often, "People make Places". It was people that Dora cared about and she was able to make herself at home with people wherever she found them, whether in Wales or Woburn Court. Unhappiness in earlier days left its scars on Dora, but it was perhaps this more than anything else that made her sensitive to the needs of those who found life difficult. She had more faith in people than she had in herself. Even when others were doubtful and they lacked faith in themselves she would encourage with a message of hope for the future. Much more could be said about Dora Slade, but the truth is that she would never have stood out in a crowd and would never have wanted to.

Her life could be summed up in a remark that she made once in a Bible Study group, **"I'm just a Jesus girl really." Not a bad epitaph though for a Christian, "I'm just a Jesus girl really."**

Dora, like Jim, was not the conventional kind of church-going Christian. Unlike Jim, she was not constantly thinking through the philosophy of Christian belief. She was more concerned with Christian behaviour. That's why for 53 years they have complemented each other in what they have shared together. Dora's life has been characterised by the enjoyment of created and creative things. The countryside, the garden, reading music and painting all brought pleasure to Dora, a pleasure that she shared with others. "The Jesus girl," like her master could look at the world around her, enjoy it, and share the lessons that she learned from it. Her sharing was more often than not done in what Wordsworth once called, "those nameless, unremembered acts of kindness and of love." Even in her later years dogged by ill-health, her gifts were shared in the practical work of doing around the church and outside. That's not to say that she could not hold her own in explaining the simple faith that she had. It's simply that her innate sensitivity allied to her relationship with Jesus Christ moved her into a way of life in which "Her actions spoke much louder than her words."

As I said at the beginning, much of what is being shared today about Dora would come as news to some people here. Dora's name will not be numbered among the well-known in the land. She would be embarrassed if it was. Christian Gellert, the writer of the second hymn we have chosen was a very famous man of his time. Theologian, philosopher, poet and saint was what the people called him. Unfortunately for most of us he wrote in German and it was left to the little-known Frances Elizabeth Cox to translate his poetry into this wonderful expression of his faith. The little-known Dora Slade, the 'Jesus girl', has done her bit in translating the life of faith into the language of living. In the spirit of her faith, we can sing:

Jesus lives! thy terrors now, Can, O Death no more appal us;
Jesus lives! By this we know Thou, O grave canst not enthrall us:
Alleluia!
Jesus lives! To him the throne High o'er heaven and earth is given;
May we go where he is gone, Live and reign with him in heaven:
Alleluia!

SMITH: Harold H. died 7th May 1994 aged 90

Our next hymn 739 is set in the form of a prayer. It was chosen by the family because it epitomises Harold Smith. What they may not know is that it was first published in a children's hymn book and its author is remembered for her Christian work among girls in West London. Happy associations with Harold. You may want to turn to it in your hymn books as I shall be using the words to focus our thoughts on the faith in which Harold lived and died.

**MAY THE MIND OF CHRIST MY SAVIOUR
LIVE IN ME FROM DAY TO DAY,
BY HIS LOVE AND POWER CONTROLLING
ALL I DO OR SAY.**

Born in 1903, Harold was brought up in the Methodist Church. His mother Ada and his father John were active members of the Osmaston Wesleyan Methodist Church in Derby. His father died when Harold was just three years old and life was not easy. Harold was nurtured in the ways of Methodism not only by his mother and grandfather who made his home with them, but also by his great uncle Walter Prentice who was a local preacher and his wife. Their family prayers made Harold feel that God was actually there with those praying. It's not surprising with that background that Harold was teaching Sunday School by the age of 15 and Sunday School Superintendent for 250 youngsters by the time he was 23.

That love and power controlling him directed the course of his life and the way he met his wife. It was while the young Monica Smith-yes, they were both Smiths before marriage-was teaching in the Senior Department of his Sunday School that the friendship turned to courtship with the dashing Superintendent.

You know what they say, "The man chases the girl until she catches him!" No matter who caught who, they have enjoyed almost 63 years of happy and fulfilling marriage.

**MAY THE WORD OF GOD DWELL RICHLY
IN MY HEART FROM HOUR TO HOUR,
SO THAT ALL MAY SEE I TRIUMPH
ONLY THROUGH HIS POWER.**

General Superintendent of four Sunday Schools, Circuit and Local Church Steward, Choir Member, Trustee, Youth Leader and so we could go on. Name it and Harold has done it in the Methodist Church. The word of God that prompted him was preached by him throughout 60 years as a Local Preacher. He certainly didn't stop preaching when he gave up taking services. He was proud of being a Methodist Preacher, a role that was much more of an adventure in earlier years.

I like the story of the two old stalwarts Dan Dennis, the non-car driver, and Harold going off to preach at different churches around Styal. Those of you who knew both of them will picture it. Harold had dropped Dan off and later discovered that Dan's preaching notes were still in the car. It was a hectic half hour before they were restored to their owner in the nick of time. **What gets me is that I can't imagine either Harold or Dan ever being stuck for something to say!**

**MAY THE PEACE OF GOD MY FATHER
RULE MY LIFE IN EVERYTHING,
THAT I MAY BE CALM TO COMFORT
SICK AND SORROWING.**

Knowing Harold only in his later years, my abiding picture will be of him, shopping bag in hand, enjoying his shopping trip to the village. He enjoyed it because it was on these trips that he met old friends and made new ones. An interesting person himself with active participation in sports, like tennis, badminton and fell walking in younger days and continued enthusiasm for football, especially with the two counties Derby and Stockport, to the end. Perhaps with the more direct contact he now has he can help Stockport to win through to the first division at last!

He became an interested person in talking to others. People found it easy to talk to him, but his interests were always secondary to theirs in any relationship. This was what made him such a good pastor, counsellor and practical support to so many people in their time of need. His concern lives on, not only in the people who have written so movingly to Monica, but in all those whose lives were touched by his friendly word.

The Centrepoint Coffee Shop has lost a valued customer but also an invaluable counsellor to all who sat down to share with him.

**MAY THE LOVE OF JESUS FILL ME,
AS THE WATERS FILL THE SEA;
HIM EXALTING, SELF ABASING—
THIS IS VICTORY.**

Many people would say that Harold's greatest witness to the Lord whom he loved was not to be found in the church, but in his career. Limits of time preclude a detailed history of Harold's pioneering work in the care of young people.

1929 appointed to Chesterfield to organise a pilot scheme in child welfare.
1935 leading a Department in Newcastle-under-Lyme entrusted with the responsibility of implementing the provisions of the Children and Young Person's Act of 1933.
1943 Superintendent Welfare Officer of the Education Department in Salford.
1948 Salford's first Children's' Officer at beginnings of the Welfare state.
1950 Children's Officer for the County of Staffordshire with responsibility for 1,100 children in care, a staff of over 300, 21 residential establishments including an Approved School, a Remand Home, and a training nursery for children's' nurses.

Harold had much to be proud of in his career. In the spirit of this verse, he found greatest joy in the large number of youngsters and their families who found in him a father figure to whom they could relate. That personal touch was not lost as many invited him to family occasions and even allowed him to undertake the role of father as he gave them away in marriage. He appreciated the unsigned Christmas card that came from, "A stranger on the Shore".

**MAY I RUN THE RACE BEFORE ME,
STRONG AND BRAVE TO FACE THE FOE,
LOOKING ONLY UNTO JESUS
AS I ONWARD GO.**

Two words came to my mind as I thought about Harold in the context of this verse. Dogged and devoted.

He was dogged in his determination to succeed in the things to which he was committed in church and working life. That doggedness could be difficult, but it kept him going when others might have given up. It kept him teetotal all his life and made him very suspicious of Methodist trends that seem to chip away at a costly devotion of abstinence that requires us to put our neighbours' needs before our own.

He was devoted to his Lord and Master, Jesus Christ, who gave direction to his life. He was devoted to his partner Monica, in everything he achieved.

Monica must have known what she was letting herself in for when a night out in Derby, meant working with Harold on the family allotment while her friends were on their way to an evening, "On the town.".

Nevertheless, Monica went ahead and married Harold in 1931 and has enjoyed working on their family allotment ever since.

It has been a very large allotment touching the lives of so many people, especially youngsters in Sunday Schools and Care, but at the very centre has been their very own Audrey and much-loved son-in-law Ron.

Harold allowed others their pride in what he achieved, but he could not hide his pride in his daughter and her achievements, especially in art. That is why I asked the family to provide one of her pictures for display today. There is in this particular picture a sense of the unseen, the unrevealed.

At death, we all experience a similar sense of mystery, of the unseen, but we hold on to what we know as fact.

That a man like Harold should have devoted his life to a man like Jesus Christ has in the process provided for us the proof that such faith works in the real world.

I know that Harold would not want me to end this word thinking only of him. May I quote in conclusion the original final verse of this hymn that is not included in our hymn book.

**MAY HIS BEAUTY REST UPON ME
AS I SEEK THE LOST TO WIN,
AND MAY THEY FORGET THE CHANNEL,
SEEING ONLY HIM.**

I think that would be Harold's prayer for us now.

SMITH: Joan B. died 11th February 1989 aged 70

It is salutary to wonder what the person who has died would want on an occasion like this. What would Joan want me to say? Very little about herself, I'm sure about that.

Joan wouldn't want much said:
about her forty plus years spent working in the Methodist Church Property Division in Manchester or of how without professional qualifications, she became the respected head of the legal department.

about her community caring through all kinds of organised and personal activities.

About her service in the Methodist Church in just about every role from Sunday School teacher to Society Steward.

About her delightful sense of humour, whether doing her impression at work of Winston Churchill (which must have been a sight to behold) or simply providing a light-hearted reading of the notices at the Tuesday Fellowship in this church.

Joan wouldn't want me to say much about her, so I won't.

Joan would want me to say "Thank you":
to cousin Barbara, Geoff and the small, but loving family for their care and support.

to her much larger family of neighbours and friends from both inside and outside the church for their friendship. They helped Joan to feel a part of other families as well as her own.

to medical and nursing staff, and especially those of Ward 4c at Stepping Hill Hospital for their sensitivity in caring.

and to those very special friends, whom I won't embarrass by naming who have ministered to Joan in so many ways, especially during the last few weeks.

Joan thanked God for us all in her own prayers and would want me to say "Thank you" to you on this public occasion.

Joan would want me to say something about God, who had become very real to her in and through Jesus Christ. It was a great joy to her and to us as she stood here on Remembrance Sunday and talked about how God had used this church and its people during wartime.

A little while ago, I asked Joan for her favourite passage of scripture. She responded with "The Lord's my Shepherd, I shall not want", not because, like so many, she did not know any other passages off by heart, but because the 23rd Psalm had proved true to her experience of God. The Psalm begins with the assurance of, "The Lord's my Shepherd" and ends with the confident claim based on her faith "and I shall dwell in the house of the Lord for ever." In life and in facing death Joan proved the truth of that Psalm. What would Joan want for today links strongly with what we would want from today that might strengthen our faith for living and prepare us better for dying. We would want to give God our thanks for the ways in which Joan Smith has enriched our lives. To give thanks that through Jesus Christ we have the assurance that Joan has passed already "from death to life".

Don't make it a sad occasion, Richard, I can hear her saying. How could we? Yes, we mourn her loss in human ways, but we also celebrate a life of love lived here that continues beyond death as Joan "dwells in the house of the Lord for ever."

The three hymns chosen for today sum up Joan's faith:

13 Praise my soul the King of Heaven
70 The Lord's my Shepherd, I'll not want
212 Thine be the glory, risen conquering Son,
   Endless is the victory thou o'er death hast won

A Consecrated life, a Companion on the way and Confidence in death-that's what Joan would want me to say today.

So, I will say that!

SOUTHERN: Winifred died 23rd Sept. 1996 aged 89

A few weeks ago, I was sat with Winifred discussing her anticipated 90th birthday due on the 12th December this year. We might have been discussing her 100th because she was so well and as she put it had, "no aches or pains" It was that positive attitude that carried her through treatment for cancer at Christies nearly forty years ago and being rushed home from Benidorm for hospital treatment three years ago. Despite this she had "no aches or pains". The one problem that caused her a little distress was her hearing. There was no problem one-to-one, but she found it difficult in a crowd. It was that which held her back from entering fully into groups and social gatherings in these later years. No such problem in younger days!

Born and brought up in Earlstown, near Warrington, Winifred graduated as a teacher from Hereford College. She met and married her late husband, Len, in 1932 and they ran a newsagents shop in Blackpool, before becoming hoteliers at the Balmoral Hotel on the Promenade for the next twenty years. Winifred had a wonderful time celebrating her Golden Wedding with her family in 1982. It was three years after her husband died that she came to live closer to family in Bramhall in 1991. Children, grandchildren and great grandchildren, she loved them all. Even when her fingers were not as flexible as they used to be, she loved to knit for others and especially the scarves toys or Easter Eggs for her family. It was a great joy to Winifred when Bruce and Alison were able to come from Ross on Wye to have their daughter Caitlin baptised alongside Andy and Mandy's daughter Millie here in this church in 1994. Winifred made friends wherever she went. Many from her hotel years stayed in contact. More recently she was blessed by a special friendship with Mrs Ceri Wright her neighbour in the flats at the Coppice. The little community of the Coppice meant a great deal to Winifred as to others gathered here this morning. The many acts of kindness and consideration were appreciated not only by Winifred, but by all the family. In the flats, Truffles in the precinct, and on the benches outside the church Winifred became a cheerful and familiar morning figure.

Winifred's first commitment to Christ and his church are lost in the annals of time, but she has been deeply committed throughout her life. The Anglican Church in Blackpool and particularly the Mother's Union benefited from her involvement in it. Here it was regular Thursday morning and Sunday worship. When there were things to be done Winifred was not far from the centre of the action. In her later years she never lost her deep concern for the under-privileged. I well remember her coming to me privately after one of our Sierra Leonean protegees had spoken at a service in our church and arranging quietly to make a donation to the particular needs that he had addressed. She had a personal concern for the world-wide church.

It's particularly appropriate then that the family have chosen as one of the hymns to be sung at this service, "The Day Thou Gavest Lord is Ended." The hymn celebrates the world-wide church and its mission. Queen Victoria chose it to be sung at her Diamond Jubilee in 1897. It is particularly appropriate for a funeral service because it reminds us of the continuity between past and present and of the way in which a long life lived well can be seen as part of the ebb and flow of life.

The imagery of day and night may be no more than background to the real meaning of the hymn, but there is a sense of satisfaction in being able to say with Winifred, "The day thou gavest Lord is ended." I never tire of reminding people that one of the loveliest images about death to be found in the New Testament is when it talks about Christians, "Falling asleep in Christ." At the end of a long, full and enjoyable life lived in Christ, Winifred Southern has fallen asleep in Christ. What more could any of us want.

So, we sing the hymn 648:

The day thou gavest, Lord is ended,
The darkness falls at thy behest;
To thee our morning hymns ascended,
Thy praise shall sanctify our rest.

STUBBS: Kathleen (Kath) died 24th Sept. 1996 aged 81

There are some funeral services that I conduct where information about a person's younger days, even amongst the family, is fragmented. Kathleen Stubbs was helpful in preparing for this day. She left diary style notes for the family and for just such an occasion as this recorded in her own inimitable matter of fact fashion.

Let me quote from 1991 so that you can appreciate the flavour of the notes.

"I am nearly 76 and in case I lose my marbles or become a victim of Alzheimer's (can't spell it) Disease over the years left to me I feel I should record how I feel."

That matter-of-fact manner is illustrative of the courage and common sense that Kathleen displayed just a few short weeks ago when she was diagnosed as having cancer and not having very long to live. There was no panic, but a ready acceptance that her time had come and a desire to prepare herself and her family to cope in a positive way.

Some of us listen regularly to Sounds of the Sixties on BBC Two on Saturday morning-some even to sounds of the fifties, but few can go back to the sounds of 1915.

Stockport born and bred, her Street Sounds from 1915 penned in 1994 could keep us here for a long time as she reflected on the sounds of the Knocker-up armed with umbrella spokes on the end of a long pole with which she would knock on the bedroom window at a time agreed. The sounds of the Coal Merchant, the rag and bone man, and the lamplighter with others are recorded for posterity. Kath was an unusual youngster, doing crosswords and having her own published in the Stockport Times when she could have only been about 14 years old.

We haven't time here this afternoon to go into detail about every aspect of Kathleen's life, but on reflection I continue to marvel at how little we know about most people until they have died.

The young sports enthusiast into everything from Hockey to Table Tennis remembered being a Guide at the World Jamboree at Chester in 1928 as the highlight of her youth. Kath began work as a Junior Office worker at Hans Reynolds in Didsbury.

She rose through the ranks to become the Private Secretary to the Employment Manager, during the next 14 years. She continued to work full-time during the war years alongside doing Clerical Work for the 1940 Air Training Corps and First Aid with Air Raid Precautions. Promoted to become the Personal Assistant for Sir Roy Dobson the Managing Director of AVRO Kath travelled the North West with the Air Ministry hierarchy, meeting many famous people in the process, Sir Thomas Sopwith, Sir Frank Spriggs, and Sir Stafford Cripps to name but a few.

Nevertheless, there was no more important man in Kath's life than her late husband Roy, whom she met at a dance in 1935. They married in 1942, but Roy had joined the Grenadier Guards in 1940 and he spent most of the war years battling through North Africa, Italy including Monte Cassino, and returning home via Austria in 1946 as a Gold Sergeant. The four years apart were soon put behind them, as Pam was born in 1948 and Ian six years later. The happy family was shattered when Roy died of a heart attack at the age of 51 and as Kath put it, "I thought I would never smile again".

Smile again she did. As she says in her notes, "Time is a great healer and we adjusted our lives." Not a bad thought for the family to hold on to today. Fortunately, Kath was able to throw herself into her work at Lombard's the Finance Company to which she had gone in 1957. She retired just short of her 60th birthday as Assistant Services Manager for the North West Region.

The adjustment was helped in later years by the care and support of countless friends from the Bridge Clubs to which Kathleen belonged, but also the fellowship that she found in the life of the church.

Kathleen loved her family and they loved her. The comments that she made about them would be embarrassing to share here. The love that they have shared was never more needed when each had to cope in their own way with the news of Kath's final illness. I was pleased when without any prompting the family chose as their hymn for this funeral service:

"Who would true valour see, let him come hither".

The words come from the second part of Pilgrim's Progress in which Mr Valiant for Truth shares with Great-heart about his Pilgrim life, of the battles he has fought and won.

It is the author John Bunyan who directs the reader to come hither and take a good look at Valiant so as to see in him the picture of a courageous and victorious pilgrim.

**The first verse stresses the need for constancy in the face of discouragement,
the second describes the fearless spirit,
and the third points to the life eternal which is the pilgrim's heavenly inheritance.**

What better hymn to sum up the life and death of Kathleen Stubbs?

TATTERSALL: May died 11th March 1994 aged 84

There are still many people who assume that if you are good enough you will get into heaven. They see being a Christian as working to pay for your passage on an ocean-going liner so that the Captain of the ship will eventually land you safely on the other shore. When death comes, comments are made like, "She never did anyone any harm" or "He would do a good turn for anyone". God is viewed as holding aloft the scales of justice and weighing in the balance what we have done in this life before he will allow St. Peter to open the gates to let us in to the next life. It's a relief to me that being a Christian is nothing like that.

The Christian faith is just that. It's about faith in Jesus Christ. Especially as we look towards Good Friday, we are reminded that there on the cross as Jesus demonstrated the love of God for all his children, the scales were forever weighted in favour of the people whom Jesus Christ came to save. It's a relief to me when I come to a funeral service like this one that I do not have to weigh anyone in the balance, but simply to share something positive about the love of God.

It becomes particularly important that our emphasis at this time is upon the love of God when thinking about someone like May Tattersall who in recent years has not been well enough to respond to God by doing many of the things that Christians are supposed to do. May was born on 23 June 1909, a month before Louis Bleriot won a prize of £1,000 from the Daily Mail for being the first person to fly across the channel. Now charity walkers raise money by walking under the channel.

May was brought up in a very different world and found it very difficult to adjust to many of the changes that have taken place in our society since the second world war. It's never easy looking back to discern when May began the moves towards becoming a virtual recluse or how far that was a consequence of early aging through illness.

Certainly, things were never the same after her friend and companion Winnie, died. Winnie and May met in the 'forties' and continued their friendship until Winnie's death in 1983.

They were both life-long Methodists, but began to get involved in the life of this church after seeing an article about Pop-in in the local press. They made the effort to come down and share on a Tuesday, carrying the little canvas chair which they sat on while waiting for the bus. It was their trip out and included a visit to the Thrift Shop.

After Winnie's death efforts were made to maintain the link by ministers, members of this church and Day Centre organisers, but May went out less and less as the years went by. Inevitably in such circumstance, people ask themselves, "Could we - should we - have tried to do more?"

I would remind members of this church and others who are sharing with us in this service of something I said in a sermon entitled, "One Foot in the Grave" that I preached a couple of weeks ago.

I was talking on Mothering Sunday about caring for old people and said that we had three principles governing our relationships.

First, we have to acknowledge that all people, no matter what age, are equal in the sight of God.

Secondly, that love must be demonstrated through sacrifice in caring as we are able for the older members of our families and communities.

But the third and most important principle, is that the old, like those who are younger, should be free to make their own decisions.

The devoted love and care given to May by her neighbour Pat & her husband Al before his recent death. The caring contacts of ministers and members of this church and even the community care given through social services allowed May the freedom to make her own decisions about continuing to live alone.

As I said in my sermon, "There should be neither recriminations nor regrets when older people, just like ourselves, occasionally get it wrong".

Winnie and May used to share in their own little communion service at home. The Bibles and little booklets in the house show that May had not lost contact with her Maker.

Certainly, there is no way that our God of love would have lost contact with her. The scales were weighted in her favour from the time she said yes to Jesus Christ.

So, God's Love and her freedom did the rest, in inspiring us as we sing:

**Thine be the glory, risen conquering Son,
Endless is the victory, thou o'er death hast won.**

WENDT: Edna E. died 12th March 1998 aged 74

Edna and Maurice Wendt and my wife Carole and I, "retired" to Bramhall at the same time in 1987. Their friendship and continuing ministry have blessed all of us. I'm grateful to Maurice, the family and Ian Coverdale for inviting me to share in this service of thanksgiving for Edna.

We read from Colossians 3.12-17

"Put on then, as God's chosen ones, holy and beloved, compassion, kindness, lowliness, meekness, and patience, forbearing one another and, if one has a complaint against another, forgiving each other; as the Lord has forgiven you, so you also must forgive. And above all these put-on love, which binds everything together in perfect harmony. And let the peace of Christ rule in your hearts, to which indeed you were called in the one body. And be thankful. Let the word of Christ dwell in you richly, as you teach and admonish one another in all wisdom and as you sing psalms and hymns and spiritual songs, with thankfulness in your hearts to God. And whatever you do, in word or deed, do everything in the name of the Lord Jesus, giving thanks to God the Father through him."

This passage from the letter to the Colossians, epitomises the life and character of Edna Wendt, one of "God's chosen ones", "holy and beloved". It was Mother Theresa of Calcutta who described holiness as "Doing the will of God with a smile." Peter Dennett, a retired minister with me in the Ashton Circuit who grew up in the same part of Widnes as Edna remembers this teenager "with a lovely smile" whom he passed three times on a Sunday on her way to Frederick Street church. Many friends in writing to Maurice and the family have taken up what has become a theme, "Edna's smile". **As I wrote personally, "It didn't matter where we met, at home, church or hospital, there was a smile on her face. Even when she answered the telephone there was a smile in her voice."**

A notable attribute in times when the minister's wife was the Ansa phone! It was because Edna did the will of God with a smile, that she was beloved of God and by all of us.

This text uses clothing imagery to invite us to **"put on"**, but the funny thing is that in contrast to the famous Diana whose tragic death has been mourned so much, I can't really remember anything that Edna wore. Her clothing really was, **"compassion, kindness, lowliness, meekness and patience,"**

Everyone has their own special memory of Edna, but I can see now that totally attentive caring expression as she listened to the concerns of an elderly member of Tuesday fellowship at the end of their meeting. She had time and sometimes tears for everyone. Edna didn't have to cultivate her love of people, the patience of a pastor and the humility that made her ministry so Christ-like, it was in a profoundly Christian sense, second nature to her.

I have to admit that I have seen the gentle Edna a little angry at times. Usually, it was when she was hurting on behalf of others. She couldn't stand what she saw as injustice and she hated the bickering and occasional animosity that sometimes mars church and family life. Her solution enshrined in this text was simple, **"if one has a complaint against another, forgive each other; as the Lord has forgiven you, so you also must forgive."**

"And above all these put on love, which binds everything together in perfect harmony". The love and faith in which Edna was nurtured translated naturally into the manse after she had served her time in the manner of those days waiting to marry the love of her life, Maurice.

They have been the perfect match in a marriage of 47 years and partners in a shared ministry to countless people. Their own love of God and enjoyment of each other has radiated outwards.

Maurice and Edna's love for their own children Philip and Gillian has reached out to enfold their extended family and is being returned now in the care shown by all their family and in the joy given to them through grandchildren, Selina, Jonathan, Sarah and Vicky.

It is that same God-inspired love that has sustained the "peace of Christ" in their hearts, even when outward circumstances have made life difficult. I believe that Maurice and Edna found the key to unlock the door to peace of heart and mind many years ago in these three simple words from v15, **"And be thankful"**. I promise that I wasn't around to hear them say to each other, "Thank God for a warm bed", but I think that simple spirit of thanksgiving undergirds the contentment that they have enjoyed.

This intrepid traveller found it staggering that they had never been out of the country apart from-was it a day trip to France? They have delighted in and given thanks for the simple, but beautiful things of life, their garden, the Yorkshire Dales, the Lake District and above all each other. Their spirit of thankfulness and contentment has overflowed to others in so many ways that the stories would fill a book.

V16 begins, **"Let the word of God dwell in you richly,"**. Edna's life was the product of that word bearing fruit in daily living. A life dedicated to God and his people in her service for the church. But her great gift was that no matter whether she was presiding at church meetings, flower arranging or singing soprano with the Ionian singers or a church choir, she enjoyed what she was doing and it showed.

She, like Maurice, was not much enamoured of choruses and charismatic worship, so I'm not too sure about the "spiritual songs" bit here! Nevertheless, I'm sure that she will be singing soprano and might even raise her hands in worship with the best of them in heaven just now while she wonders about the fuss that we are making here.

Edna's epitaph and the challenge her life presents to us can be found in verse 17, **"And whatever you do, in word or deed, do everything in the name of the Lord Jesus, giving thanks to God the Father through him."**

Edna would ask for nothing more and God would want nothing less of those, who like Edna, have chosen to follow Jesus in this life and know that we shall be with Him in the next.

Many words have been used in speaking of Edna's faith and life. Sarah, a granddaughter, has used only a few words in the prayer that she has written, but she sums it up so simply.

She will read it for us now as a prayer.

Dear God, your world is so wonderful the heaven and earth and sky.
There was one lady who was loving and caring and always joyful.
She was my Grandma, of course. She had a heart of gold.
She always smiled and was happy. Please send the message on.
We all love her and miss her. The world is so different without her.
Please look after her in heaven as well as you did on earth
and make sure she looks after us all day long. Amen

There's also a picture of Grandma inside a heart and a picture of Sarah saying, "I love you Grandma and miss you."

Hymn 484 verses 1, 3, 4 & 5

Angel voices, ever singing round thy throne of light
Angel harps, for ever ringing, rest not day or night;
Thousands only live to bless thee, And confess thee
Lord of Might.

WENDT: Revd S Maurice died 24th June 1998 aged 76

      I think that my wife Carole echoed the immediate reaction of many of us as when we heard the news of Maurice's death. "Well," she said, "they weren't apart very long." Just four months ago we were in this church thanking God for the life and witness of Edna Wendt and we gather again now to reflect on the life and ministry of Maurice Wendt. Edna & Maurice in their life together epitomised the scripture, "and the two shall become one". Married for 47 years, they remembered and celebrated their first date fifty years on. They say that after many years together that you become like your partner. Certainly, much that we said in that service about Edna, "doing the will of God with a smile", her compassion, thankfulness, humility and love might be repeated here as we remember with thanksgiving Maurice Wendt.

      As a focus for our thanksgiving, I thought we might helpfully use words addressed to Maurice when he was ordained by the Methodist Church to the ministry of word and sacrament. The presiding minister handed a Bible to Maurice and the others being ordained with him and made the following declaration, "Take thou authority to fulfil the office of a minister in the Church of Christ." He went on to say, "In the Name of our Lord Jesus Christ, the only Head of the Church, I hereby declare you to be ordained to the office of the Holy Ministry." And then he urged all who had been ordained, "Brethren, give heed unto reading, exhortation, and doctrine. Think upon the things contained in the Holy Bible which we have now delivered unto you. Be diligent; never be unemployed, never be triflingly employed. Take heed unto yourselves and to the doctrine; for by so doing, you shall both save yourselves and them that hear you. Let each of you be to the flock of Christ a shepherd; feed them, devour them not. Hold up the weak, heal the sick, bind up the broken, bring again the outcasts, seek the lost. Be so merciful, that you be not too remiss; so minister discipline, that you forget not mercy; that when the Chief Shepherd shall appear you may receive the never-fading crown of glory; through Jesus Christ our Lord. Amen."

(Ordination Service 1936-Book of Offices)

"Brethren, give heed unto reading, exhortation, and doctrine. Think upon the things contained in the Holy Bible which we have now delivered unto you."

Maurice had a problem with theological labels like evangelical and radical, conservative, charismatic or liturgical. His was a Bible based ministry and life, but he would have been horrified to have been labelled conservative evangelical, much less charismatic. It was a shock to his system on our shared arrival in Bramhall to discover that I was both! It was a standing joke between us that the spirit would move him to raise his hands in the air in worship. It was a tribute to his love for children and a willingness to identify with them that he and Edna would be as animated as anyone in the congregation when action songs including raising hands were called for. Maurice accepted that such overt reactions were biblical, but as expressions of his own faith they were not for him.

His preaching and teaching bore the light touch of the lover of the Bible who shared in a simple way the truths that he discovered there. One of my great joys as a minister here in Bramhall when we started the 9.15 services was to be able to sit in with many of you on Maurice's ministry. He delighted in the great traditional hymns of Wesley, shot through with allusions to scripture, and Watts glorying in the created world. We were refreshed in heart and mind by a gracious leading of worship, a simplicity of style, authentic prayer, and sermons that communicated his own love of life.

Who can forget his carefully observed illustrations from flower and field, from garden and countryside, that took us around the Lake District or the Yorkshire Dales and back again to the Bible story to link up with one of our Saviour's own stories?

Like John Wesley the reader of many books, Maurice was a man of one book and that book was the Bible, but he read life like a book and shared his understanding of Christian living in words and deeds that have blessed us all.

"Be diligent; never be unemployed, never be triflingly employed. Take heed unto yourselves and to the doctrine; for by so doing, you shall both save yourselves and them that hear you. Let each of you be to the flock of Christ a shepherd; feed them, devour them not. Hold up the weak, heal the sick, bind up the broken, bring again the outcasts, seek the lost."

Maurice was a competent administrator who made time for those things that needed to be done, but it was in the pastoral ministry that he excelled. He revelled in the opportunities that his so-called retirement gave him to "do just the bits of ministry he liked". Those "bits" were always to do with people and the people in all the Circuits where he served loved him for it.

Born and brought up in the countryside near Widnes, he attended the Cronton Methodist Church, was educated at Wade Deacon Grammar School and worked for some years in the Runcorn offices of ICI before entering the Methodist ministry. He began in 1945 as a pre-collegiate probationer in the Kidderminster & Stourport Circuit before training at Hartley Victoria College from 1947-49. In circuits as widespread as Holyhead, Crewe, Wellington (Shropshire), Newbury, Reading (where he was also a Forces Chaplain) and Chichester & Bognor (where he was Superintendent & Hospital Chaplain) back to Northwich as superintendent, people talk about his care and concern for them personally. He enjoyed visiting even when it meant visiting plus mowing the lawn weekly for one older lady.

His small pastoral section of Dairyground here in Bramhall quickly expanded to incorporate Tuesday Fellowship and Coffee Morning contacts, but in fact as everyone discovered both Maurice and Edna had a ready ear for anyone with any kind of concern.

As for so many pastors the bond of confidentiality precludes publicity, but there are many here today who if asked could bear testimony to the importance of Maurice's pastoral work to their own life's journey.

Having ministered to so many people in a lifetime of service, Maurice could hardly get over the love and concern expressed by so many to him during the past few months as he coped first with the loss of his beloved partner in all things, Edna, and then his own illness and hospitalisation. Maurice was just so grateful to all of you and many others who in a variety of practical and compassionate ways ministered to the one who continued his own ministry of prayer for others even from his hospital bed. He never lost that sense of humour which in the early days invited his beloved Edna to join this little man on his huge motorbike that he claimed was safe for two. He was amused by the hospital staff using his middle name, Stanley, until we had it changed on the admission card and ward board. Nearing the end, he gave his consultants that knowing quizzical look of his when they gathered round his bed and with a twinkle in his eye described them to others as "the three wise men."

It can be a great sadness to some ministers in later life when the demands made upon their time in earlier days are seen to have blighted relationships with their children and sometimes even their partners in marriage. Edna and Maurice felt blessed in having a supportive and caring family nearby in these latter years. Having the two children Philip & Gillian, son-in-law, Jonathan and all the family around continued to be a great comfort and joy to Maurice, especially during the last few weeks and days. Our prayers are with you in your double loss. We mourn with you, even as we celebrate the life and ministry of your father and grandfather Maurice Wendt, for we too have lost someone we found easy to love.

I think that Maurice the friend and family man would be content to see us gathered here as his friends and family. Maurice the Methodist Minister would rejoice in the knowledge that he has kept his ordination vows and fulfilled, **"the office of a Minister in the Church of Christ."** He and we rest assured in the knowledge that for him **"the Chief Shepherd" has appeared and Maurice re-united with his partner Edna has received, "the never-fading crown of glory; through Jesus Christ our Lord. Amen."**

WHARTON: Thomas (Tom) died 25th Dec. 1993 aged 96

The family have chosen one hymn for today's service whose central theme is suffering. I didn't ask them why they thought it particularly appropriate on the death of this grand old man at the age of 96.

> O LOVE that wilt not let me go,
> I rest my weary soul in thee:
> I give thee back the life I owe,
> That in thine ocean depths its flow
> May richer, fuller be.

Certainly, there was a degree of suffering attached to those early years as the oldest child of six, born to James and Margaret Wharton and brought up to work in the family business. In common with so many of his generation he began work half-time at the age of 13. Groceries had to be packed and orders delivered by handcart. Bad enough with shop hours of 8.00 a.m. to 9.00 p.m., but in Burnley, noted for its hills, the shop just happened to be at the bottom of a hill! As many people who have avoided it say, "Hard work never killed anybody." It wasn't the hard work that Tom regretted, but the missed opportunity to further his education at grammar school and make the kind of career choices that we take for granted in these days.

Tom saw real suffering in the first world war, when against the wishes of his parents he volunteered and joined the Royal Army Medical Corps to serve in France, Belgium and Germany. That war to end all wars left ten million dead, three-quarters of a million from Britain alone. We who have only seen newsreel pictures and photographs can only wonder about the reality of trench warfare and the use of poisonous gas. Tom was there as an impressionable young man helping the casualties and trying to come to terms with the horror and brutality of it all. No wonder he like so many others who returned found it difficult to talk about his experiences.

There was joy and suffering too in married life. Tom, began attending Brunswick Methodist Sunday School in his early teens. Later he was to become a teacher there and Superintendent of the Junior Dept. There in 1914, he met Annie who became his wife in 1922. Ten years later they were blessed by the birth of their daughter Dorothea, which was a prelude to a dramatic change in their family life. Tom's father closed the business in 1933 at the height of the depression and Tom moved with his family to Manchester where he became manager of a billiard hall for the next 30 years in Burton Road, Withington.

Tom, for me, tended to devalue his work of running a billiard hall for such a long time. Perhaps if he had been encouraged to see himself as a paid youth leader who kept young ruffians like myself who frequented such places off the street, he might have felt happier about the work that he spent much of his life doing. Nevertheless, his work enabled him to join Dorothea in giving devoted care to his wife who was diagnosed as suffering from Multiple Sclerosis in 1939 and who eventually died in 1966.

Tom was able to enjoy a second family as he shared a home with Colin and Thea Duff and his grandchildren Helen and Peter. As he wrote in his diary which I am looking forward to reading in full, "How fortunate I am to have such a wonderful family!" The family was his joy, but the sadness and frustration came again with increasing deafness and loss of sight.

It was in these later years that Carole and I came to know Tom.

I can still see the smile on his face when we had the loop system installed in this church and he could hear the service in full for the first time in many years. As our elder statesman he would sit in state at the end of each service and wait for his courtiers, usually women you will note, to come and have a word and be sent away with a beaming smile. So much more might be said about this faith-full grand old man Tom Wharton, but I think his life and faith is summed up in the hymn the family have chosen.

**O LOVE that wilt not let me go,
I rest my weary soul in thee:
I give thee back the life I owe,
That in thine ocean depths its flow
May richer, fuller be.**

George Matheson said that this hymn was the fruit of his suffering. Perhaps that is why it sums up Tom's faith so well in sharing:

v1 love that holds us-even when surrounded by the tragedy of war.

v2 light that follows us-the blind poet Matheson like Tom could see

v3 joy that seeks us through pain-joy the flip- side of suffering coin.

v4 cross that lifts us-suffering coped with through the cross of Jesus.

Suffering coped with throughout his life, strengthened Tom's faith.

May this hymn do the same for us all as we sing.

WHITCHURCH: John F. died 22nd May 1992 aged 58

I, like many other people, have said of John Whitchurch, that he was a rough diamond. When I began to think about him in preparing for this service, I realised that the hardness that relates to a diamond had little place in John's life.

John was soft at heart and in all his actions. He wasn't a Jack: - he was a John with some of the traits of the Apostle from whom he received his name.

JOHN THE APOSTLE linked the coming of Jesus Christ into the world with the God who created the world with the well-known words, "In the beginning was the word and the word was with God and the word was God." The God who created the world was the God who was in Christ. John Whitchurch loved the creator and the Christ. The beauty and design found in the created world was never separated from the spiritual.

John Whitchurch saw reflected in creation the love of God. So, Robin, his son writing from Canada says, "I very much regret that I am unable to attend the celebration of John's life today but will, at the actual time, even though many thousands of miles away, be walking on the shore. It will be sunrise - a favourite time of his - and the silence of the fresh awakening of the day will only be broken by the birds and creatures in the marsh. Until we meet again - so long John."

John will appreciate that. Even during his last few days looking out from the hospital ward at Stepping Hill, John was enjoying the sunrise and sunset and planning further photography of the beauty he found in it. It must have been a delight to be with John drifting along a canal on a narrow-boat and sharing his child-like enjoyment of the simple things of life. It was fitting that Pam and John were able to enjoy such a holiday in the past few weeks. John wondered at God's creation before he worked in it.

It was that wonder which made his chosen work as a gardener such a joy to him and influenced others with whom he shared.

JOHN THE APOSTLE was not an up-front leader.

We find John in the Gospels with Peter and James his brother as part of the inner circle of disciples who were with Jesus. Peter becomes the leader of the young church, but John is more of a back-room boy. He quietly lives alongside Jesus and learns by being with him and sharing his company. John is described in the Gospels as, "the disciple whom Jesus loved." To Peter, Jesus entrusts the church, but to John, Jesus entrusted the care of his mother Mary as he hung dying on the cross.

John Whitchurch was the kind of person who loved and cared for Pam's mum, Norah in very practical ways during her later years. The love that was learned from Christ overflowed from John into the lives of others from his early days in the church. It didn't matter whether John was leading the Venture Scouts or tending the church gardens free of charge, it was his easy-going nature that bore a witness as important as his practical work.

As one person has written of him, "Nothing was ever too much or too difficult for him, if he could find the time (and somehow he always did)." Family, friends and the church have been blessed through the willing love and uncomplaining service that John gave.

JOHN THE APOSTLE

Learned that love was the most important thing in the world. It's said that when John the Apostle was being carried into the church at Ephesus in old age, he was still saying to the young men who carried him,

"Little children, love one another."

John Whitchurch too had learned the lesson of love. No, he wasn't really a rough diamond, because God's love made him soft at the centre. He would certainly be embarrassed at the thought of being compared to an Apostle, because John was one who recognised only too well his own short-comings.

Nevertheless, whatever mistakes John made in his life, they were made in the cause of love and not hate. That is why he was held in such affection by family, friends, church, and those with whom he worked. His love was offered freely to all and no-one could have spent time with him especially over these past few months without realising that they were in the presence of a man who was at peace with his God and with his neighbour.

Perhaps this is why his favourite hymn was that sung by the Manx fishermen. A hymn that acknowledges God in creation and the peace that Jesus gives in the storms of life. It remembers family and others' needs in Creation.

The final verse of HYMN 346 could have been written for John.

"SOW IN OUR HEARTS THE SEEDS OF THY DEAR LOVE, THAT WE MAY REAP CONTENTMENT, JOY, AND PEACE; AND WHEN AT LAST OUR EARTHLY LABOURS CEASE, GRANT US TO JOIN THY HARVEST HOME ABOVE."

WROE: Rev'd John H. died 18th Jan. 1988 aged 76

Revd John H. Wroe died suddenly on Monday 18th January, the day that began the Octave of Prayer for Christian Unity. His life and ministry illustrated the chosen text from 1 John 4: 7-21 **"Beloved let us love one another; for love is of God, and he who loves is born of God and knows God."**

Born in 1911, and brought up in Liverpool of a non-church attending family, John realised the love that God had for him in his teenage years and responded by making a commitment to Christ in a Liverpool Mission Hall one Young People's Sunday. After early nurture in Liverpool, and a year at Cliff College, where one of his cherished memories was to be chosen as one of the pall bearers at the funeral of the great Samuel Chadwick, he trained for the Methodist Ministry at Hartley Victoria College, beginning a B.D. degree which he eventually completed in Circuit.

Any person born and brought up in Liverpool is almost inevitably going to be a football fan. John was no exception and became an almost fanatical supporter of Everton F.C. It was also in Liverpool where he first met the young lady Margaret Scott Farrier (Peggy) who had moved there from Tyneside and who was later to have to wait for what seemed an eternity before the Methodist Conference, in its wisdom decreed that they were allowed to marry. In fact, John spent three years as Chaplain at Truro School after his college training before that happy wedding day. After marriage, John and Peggy came to the Hazel Grove and Poynton Circuit for a welcome meeting in Poynton, the very place where John took his last service on the Sunday morning before his death. After a year in Poynton, the Wroe's spent three years in Wales before returning to the Manchester & Stockport District to spend five years in Ashton-under-Lyne. There followed two periods of seven years each on the Lancashire coast at Morecambe and Blackpool with a three-year spell at another Methodist School - Woodhouse Grove - in between.

Then came an outstanding ministry in Bramhall, before they concluded their active ministry back in the Liverpool area at Crosby. It was a great joy for John, Peggy, and one of the churches which had been blessed by their ministry when they were able to return almost ten years ago to retire among friends at Bramhall. Retirement for John, as Peggy soon discovered, was simply a transition into a less regimented but no less enthusiastic activity. John's love of life and people communicated itself in painting and political discussion, in bowling club and badminton matches. He loved to share with all kinds of people but more especially God's people. He was active in Probus, the Fellowship of the Kingdom, the District Men's Luncheon Club, Art Group and Pop-In and countless other meetings where he was a welcome host, guest or regular speaker. He was always a great encourager to his brethren in the ministry and a sensitive helper of those he worked alongside in his retirement,

Daughters Valerie and Dorothy shared their father with a much larger family. They helped to keep John in touch with the youngsters he loved so much. What brought so many of those "youngsters" back at such short notice from as far away as Scotland for the funeral service? As one commented, "He didn't preach at us - he loved us into the Kingdom of God and into becoming church members." That love for people of all ages undergirded his ministry and was the message he shared, sometimes at length, in his preaching, His preaching tinged with that sense of humour that permeated every aspect of John's personality continued to be appreciated as he journeyed to churches large and small throughout the District and beyond during his "retirement". The name John is associated with "the disciple whom Jesus loved."

John Wroe was a disciple whom Jesus and all of us loved and we thank God for his love shared with us through John's fifty years of ministry in his beloved Methodist Church. Many people were inspired as a packed church gave thanks for the life and ministry of John Wroe and we pray God's continuing blessing on Peggy and the family who in so many ways shared that ministry with him.

YOUNG: Sheila M. died 19th May 1995 aged 86

Last Saturday, I was at Wembley watching my team ,Manchester United, lose in the Cup Final to Everton. On Sunday afternoon, I was surprised to discover that Sheila Young had once umpired International Hockey matches on that same Wembley pitch. Once again, those of us who only knew Sheila in her later years that were dogged with ill-health have to use our imagination to discover the real Sheila who led such a full and active life.

Sheila was born in Dublin in 1908 and brought up in Cork with her three elder sisters. Her father, a shipping manager, was sent by his firm to Ireland and became a prominent member of the community. During the earlier 'troubles' in Ireland in the early 1920's, the family were ordered into their garden at gunpoint and had to watch their possessions and their house being burned to the ground. Mr. Young sent his family back to England, but despite the threats to his life he stayed on in Ireland by himself, with a courage and determination that was to characterise Sheila 's later life.

The young Sheila qualified as a P.E. teacher, teaching first in the south of England before moving to Carmarthen in South Wales. She found time to play hockey, qualify as an international umpire, captain a thriving Guide Company, become District Commissioner and train potential Guide Officers.

I must let just one person speak on the behalf of countless young people whose lives were influenced for good by Sheila's enthusiasm and devotion.

A Christmas card received last Christmas from New Zealand reads,

"Dear Sheila- always been Miss Young to me-and if it is not too late to say so-I would like you to know-and possibly you realise-that you were the most influential person who 'set me along the road'. I look back on the Guiding and Cadet Training as being-if you like-'the making of me'-thanks to you-and even now, I look back and wonder at your wonderful energy, initiative and dedication-for which I thank you. Sorry, not meant to be a speech, but please know that you are on the top pedestal.

With Love Thelma".

That same energy and dedication had Sheila teaching at two schools about thirty miles apart during the war and driving ambulances during air raids at night. The driving stood her, and Mary, in good stead when they met up at Bangor Normal College in 1950. She taught Mary to drive and they began a friendship that has meant so much to them both in the forty-odd years since that time. The friendship was sustained as both of their careers took them in different directions. It was not until 1966 that Mary and Sheila worked again together in the same College at Didsbury when Sheila took charge of a hostel of 250 students and lectured part-time in the Music & Drama Department.

It's difficult for many of us who only knew Sheila in her later years to imagine her at 50. She still led camps for students, drove a series of motor caravans around Europe, and even played hockey, albeit in the goal for the Penistone ladies' hockey team.

Even when she retired from full-time work in 1968, she was still throwing herself, quite literally, into the part-time work of the drama department. Two years of voluntary work with disabled children at Bethesda School, Cheadle, followed her retirement from paid employment in 1974. Sheila and Mary finally retired to Bramhall in 1977.

Sheila was a confirmed Anglican, but she and Mary found a new spiritual home in Bramhall Methodist Church, having been welcomed on their first visit by Stan Nicol.

Old age did not stop her doing what she could during those years in the church here, from organising the Tuesday Fellowship Car Rota, helping with Coffee Mornings and even with babysitting for younger families as long as her health held out. The devoted love and care which had so characterised her life was repaid in full by Mary as in later years Sheila struggled to keep going. With Mary's help, Sheila attended church worship regularly until her recent final illness.

By one of those happy decisions, she finally agreed to let go of her loyalty to the Anglican church and become a member here on the first of January this year. Her health may have faltered, but her faith didn't.

It would be wrong to pretend that Sheila was a Saint. She had a mind of her own and could decide for others as well as for herself on occasions! Like most good umpires and referees she could be inclined to run the 'game' off the field as well as on it!

What shone through was that love and concern for others that is at the very heart of our Christian faith and for which so many people have good cause to be thankful.

For all that we have said about her I think that she would be quite happy with the recent comment of a former colleague as her epitaph, "She was such fun".

It's hard to have fun at a funeral, but I don't think Sheila will be sad now. I think a picture of her with a heavenly hockey stick organising those who want to play as well as those who don't, would be a truer picture of her than that which many of us saw in old age.

Just remember, "She was such fun!"

MEMORIES OF OTHERS REMEMBERED

"She was such fun!" might have provided an appropriate final word for a book such as this, but like preachers from time immemorial, I was prompted to carry on beyond the original scope of this presentation.

In the spirit of Hebrews 11, when talking about the heroes of the faith and verse 32 in particular: "And what more should I say? For time would fail me to tell of, Gideon, Barak, Samson, Jephthah, of David and Samuel and the prophets-…."

Obviously, there were additional family and personal tributes shared in some funeral services that are not included here. Other shorter services were conducted at the Crematorium or the Graveside. In the brief notes that follow about other people, I have tried to isolate at least one memory that might be of interest, especially to family and friends who remember these names.

So, as Jimmy Cricket the comedian used to say, "There's more!", but here much more briefly we share some lessons learned from others of our generation associated with Bramhall and the church saints who have died in the faith of Jesus Christ.

"We will remember them!"

ALDRED: Leslie died aged 84

A draughtsman with GEC and later technical officer with ICI, who lived in Stretford, but was not a Manchester United supporter. He was too busy with cycling, tennis, his vegetable garden and helping others.

BARKER: Dorothy died 27th February 1988 aged 86

Who welcomed us to Bramhall with a Christmas card and gift accompanied by the message: "Please no acknowledgment." Words that became her epitaph a few months later as we recorded her sacrificial care of Norman her husband and of others in need.

BARKER: Norman Cyril died 25th April 1988 aged 94

The active gentle man of younger years, who was at peace with the care received from others, including his late wife, Dorothy. He coped with the illness that dulled his senses by finding pleasure in the simple enjoyment of life and thanksgiving for kindnesses received.

BARRIE: Denis St Clair died 2nd February 1991 aged 76

"A true gentleman in every sense of the word", whose life was punctuated by war service in North Africa; commitment to the scouting organisation, receiving the Chief Scout's award and being rewarded by recruiting Cordelia his lifelong love and wife from the Guides.

BLAND: June died 30th October 1994 aged 56

Brought up in BMC, a social caring person, danced her way to bronze, silver and gold medals, but she claimed her most important award came in 1961 when Peter 'danced' her into BMC for their marriage!

BRENNON: Harry died 1ˢᵗ June 1993 aged 60

An accountant who knew his own mind and would let you know it too, but always with a redeeming droll sense of humour.

BRIERS: Raymond U. died 31ˢᵗ July 1996 aged 82

Ray was a sportsman, who drove through the war with the Tank Brigade, landing in France on D-Day plus two, the proud recipient of a notation signed personally by Montgomery.

Post-war he claimed that his one-man van company had its first office in a telephone kiosk outside Strangeways Prison.

BROWN: Mabel died 6ᵗʰ November 1990 aged 92

Much of Mabel's life was spent 'in Service' to use that quaint phrase of old, Never blessed with much of the world's goods, she continued to serve her Master and other people in so many ways, but when asked how she was in later years she would respond, "I'm fine, but I just need two new feet."

To hear Mabel sharing about her special 90ᵗʰ birthday celebration of a flight to London to see the sights, was to fly with her, knowing that the state of her feet didn't really hold her back.

BURNEY: Mark died 25ᵗʰ September 1992 aged 91

Birkenhead Housing Manager "who could turn his hand to anything". When asked, "Do you like gardening?" He responded, "No, but I do like a nice garden!"

BURNHAM: Lily died 3rd April 1991 aged 80

Lily played hockey for the Moss Side Baptist's hockey team. As reported in the 1930's, "Battling Lily Burnham smote the ball with such ferocity that the goalkeeper has not yet been born that would have saved it." Battlers are not easy to live with, but Lily who ran Guides, Sunday School and Youth Club into her 70's was much loved too.

CASTELL: Jean died 20th May 1996 aged 82

"When war broke out" Jean enlisted with a friend in the Women's Land Army and made many friends on farms throughout Cheshire engaging in the back-breaking, but rewarding work of farming.

COGHLAN: Robert (Bob) died 15th Sept. 1990 aged 82

Bob was a grateful person: grateful to family; grateful to friends at Birch House and groups like the British Legion; above all grateful to God. The death of his wife Eve in a tragic road accident 28 years ago stayed with him, but it didn't stop him from talking about the friendship he found here in this church as a 'Coming Home'.

COLBRAN: Richard (Dick) G. died 4th August 1996

Family Address and tributes.

COOKE: Louise died 28th April 1992 aged 81

Louise was totally involved in the church during younger days in Liverpool, becoming a Sunday School Teacher. In later years she shared that same enthusiasm for life and other people through the Brookdale Centre in Bramhall.

COOPER: Leslie died 2nd February 1990 aged 61

Though Leslie loved his Bible and lived by it, he did not attend church regularly. As an accountant, he would be happy with Romans 14:12 "Every one of us then, will have to give an account of himself to God."

DUMBELL: Walter died 18th August 1995 aged 80

Walter was known as the 'flying gasman' who cycled everywhere on his meter reading rounds and refused free driving lessons when they were offered to him. If you picture the 'Last of the Summer Wine' on bikes you will share some of the fun of the 'Fanatics' in later years.

FORD: Vivienne (V.M.) died 25th June 1997 aged 89

Born into the sweated labour of women in London's East End, the happiest years of Vivienne's life were spent in supporting her family as a Secretary in the glamorous world of the BBC.

She brought the same enthusiasm and administrative gifting in retirement to the work of a school secretary.

GREEN: Maud died 1st December 1994 aged 94

Born and brought up in Stockport Methodism. After marriage to Frank, a farmer on the Isle of Man, she played the organ at the ancient Anchorage Church, Agneash for over thirty years.

HAIGH (HAY): Florence M. died 2nd Dec. 1992 aged 77

Florence was a rare combination of Mary and Martha in quiet faithfulness and practical caring. In the words of Anna Waring from a lesser-known hymn, "Content to fill a little space, if God be glorified.

HALL: Muriel E. died 25th June 1988 aged 80 years

Muriel enjoyed an active life within the church and supporting the Guide movement whilst bringing up a large and loving family. Later years saw the active younger woman wheelchair-bound as an older lady needing all the love and care that her family and friends could share with her.

HALLWORTH: (Joe)seph died 14th Sept. 1989 aged 77

Known as a friendly man, working with the Trustee Savings Bank and earning a reputation for 'liking to say yes' in both church and community life. He celebrated his 52nd wedding anniversary, with Phyllis and the family just the week before he died.

HARPER: Evelyn M. died 22nd November 1996 aged 85

Born in Stretford, married to Tom, opened a greengrocery shop in Cheadle Hulme in 1963. A year later their only son Kenneth was killed in a car crash at the age of 21. On retirement in 1978 moved to Bramhall, but four years later her beloved Tom died.

Countless clubs and organisations including the British Legion benefitted from Evelyn's quiet enthusiasm. Here in older age, she simply belonged and was faithfully present in worship on Sundays. Her faith was summed up in her favourite hymn, "Take my life and let it be, consecrated Lord to thee, Take my moments and my days, Let them flow in ceaseless praise."

HATTON: Kath(leen) died 20th August 1994 aged 73

A confessed shopaholic, who loved clothes and always dressed well, for her husband of 51 years and because that's who she was, careful and correct in faith, worship, and life. She delighted to sing along with TV's 'Songs of Praise" on a Sunday evening.
No doubt, she and others in heaven would be singing along with us a month later on the 25th September as SOP's largest crowd ever of over 40,000 sang the hymns of faith from Old Trafford.

HIGGINS: Sid(ney) died 12th February 1994 aged 72

Practical man as both a Market Gardener and School Caretaker. Loved a bargain at auctions and car boot sales, but reckoned that the real bargain of his life was his wife Ethel of almost fifty years and their family.

HOBSON: Harry (Henry S.) died 1989 aged 88

Married Marion and took on a baker's shop on the same weekend in 1929. Said to have survived the depression and war years, not by running a business, but by caring about people. A Christian gentleman throughout his life, we have been blessed by him in Bramhall for just two years.

JACOB: Rose A. died 9th January 1990 aged 75

From 1914 to 1978 Rose lived a lifetime in the London of the blitz and the air raid shelter; of Royal occasions and great events and friends were regaled with such stories. Alan's love of birds and her love of gardens and God's creation brought her closer to God in the north.

KELLETT: Trevor J. died June 1997 aged 61

Bramhall born and bred, Trevor worked in the Stockport tax office, eventually becoming an Inspector. Met his wife Joan there and married her on 1st September 1959. She was promptly transferred to another tax office! The Bramhall & Woodford community benefitted from this DIY 'craftsman' linked with Brookdale, Bridge, Chess and Golf Clubs, later caring with the Community Council and as he visited for the Civil Service retirement Fellowship.

LAKE: William (Bill) H. died 26th Jan. 1997 aged 84

Immaculate in dress, always with a tie, and meticulous in his work for twenty-five years at Avro, which earned him a gold watch! Brought up in Levenshulme, Methodism defined Bill's attitude to life.

LAMB: Lily V. died 1st January 1991 aged 93

Last survivor of a family of twelve children who sang her faith in a number of choirs and transferred here from Wigton Road Methodist Church, Carlisle, fourteen years ago. This cheerful 93-year-old found pleasure in baking and even more pleasure in giving away what she had baked. Many friends in her beloved Tuesday Fellowship benefitted from her generosity.

MATTISON: J. Leslie died 20th January 1991

Lifelong Methodist whose banking experience helped programme his commitment as a treasurer and trustee.

MELLOR: Joe (Joseph) died 17th Feb. 1995 aged 79

Methodist music-maker played saxophone & clarinet in dance bands and loved wife of almost fifty-one years Muriel and family, plus the hmour of Morcambe & Wise, hopefully in that order.

NAYLOR: John E. died 27th June 1996 aged 65

A Yorkshireman through and through, playing cricket in local leagues and even once for his beloved county of Yorkshire.

The 'grit' that carried him through his mature student's education to become a training officer, motivated him in sport, geology, wood working & restoration as well as family life.

NOBLE: Marjorie E. died 4th August 1989 aged 79

Marjorie is derived from Margaret associated with a pearl. A pearl hidden in the oyster of a librarian at John Rylands Library, but treasured by those she befriended in the church and community.

NORBURY: Anne died 27th October 1996 aged 87

Grew up in Newlands, Scotland, Anne met her husband Bill in the Isle of Man whilst on holiday with her sister Marion, while Bill was with his brother Harold. Anne married Bill in 1935 and later Harold married Marion!

Anne moved to Bramhall after her husband died in 1980 and became a member of BMC, helping develop the Thrift Shop in its early years.

PICKFORD: Ada died aged 89

After holding almost every office and a life-time of practical service in Woodsmoor Methodist Church, Ada shared in writing how grateful she was for the friends at BMC who adopted her and cared for her when she moved into Hillbrook Grange.

POTTS: May died 6th June 1996 aged 88

Began work as a machinist at the age of thirteen and married childhood friend John in 1936. Life for 'Auntie May' as she was known revolved round the church.

Comedien compere John and singer May formed a concert party, entertaining widely and with radio performances. Latterly, May had more clubs than a golfer, with Monday Club at Woodford through to Friday Club at St. Michaels's.

ROBERTS: Peter J. died 25th June 1991 aged 62

I never went to see Peter without being asked at some stage, "And you, how are you?" A question not about the church or the work, but a very personal question which allowed us to pray through the answer.

"And you, how are you?" is a question for us all to ask and to answer.

SMITH: Lily died February 1996 aged 64

Fitness fanatic, flower lover, Francophile and family lover of faith summed up Lily Smith's life as long as you added a Yorkshire woman from Pudsey.

All of these things and more her devoted family talked about for a month to the heavily sedated Lily during her final illness.

SOUTHERN: John L. B. died 26th April 1997 aged 61

A banker who cared. A treasurer who was treasured wherever he travelled after his early years with family at the Balmoral Hotel, Blackpool where he met and married Pam. Son Andy's heartfelt poetic tribute, is summed up in the repeated words: "That was my Dad!"

SULLIVAN: John died 18th July 1990 aged 75

An engineer in earlier days doing what he enjoyed doing, working with his hands, but later made many friends as the owner of a newsagents shop on the corner of Bramhall Lane and Wellington Road South.

Churchgoing links tenuous, partly because of a lifetime commitment to the scouting movement.

WARD: Annie (Nan) died 23rd April 1993 aged 92

Left school at the age of twelve to work as a machinist in the garment trade. Continued to use her dressmaking skils throughout her life as with her piano playing nurtured as a youngster by a Sunday School teacher, which led Nan and her family to enjoy a very full life with choir participation, solo singing and dancing at Walsh's Academy.

WHITE: Doris E. died 17th May 1988 aged 78

Background family life in Wellingborough allowed the Doris of later years to believe that in the scriptures, God is not just telling us what the divine nature is like, but in Jesus Christ showing how much God cares about us.

WORTHINGTON: J. E.(Ted) died 3rd Apr. 1994 aged 72

Moved about the country as an Air Traffic Engineer and as a true Yorkshireman, brought up in Hull enjoyed his cricket, rugby gardening, but unusually cooking too! Active in the Village Club, he was its Chair for three years and was known to escape occasionally to his beloved Yorkshire Dales. Less well-known, is that he used to escape here also to sit quietly and pray in Bramhall Methodist Church.

WRIGHT: Bertha died 28th January 1997 aged 89

After an unsettled childhood due to the early death of her mother, Bertha as a teenager married her work colleague, Fred and they enjoyed sixty years of a settled married life. Along with their church, Old time dancing was their great love-they danced their way through life and raised large sums of money for the British Legion.

SPEAKING PERSONALLY

People of my generation have attended far too many funeral services and now we are even being encouraged to plan our own! It is being suggested to an increasing number of friends that we should include in our will, or at least prepare what we would like at our funeral service for our family and/or friends to make the proper arrangements.

As we have shared already, family and friends contribute in a number of ways to every funeral service. Those leading the service, whether they know the person who has died or not are often blessed by what is shared by others and sometimes that sharing is done within the service itself as a member of the family, or close friend supplements the service with a personally presented eulogy.

Their voices too are heard in the choice of scripture readings and the hymns chosen for the service, but also in the music being played. That music ranges from the theme tune of favourite "Soaps" through a complete genre of pop songs, from ballads to 'Punk' right through to the Classical compositions, loved by so many as providing the right mood for the occasion.

Well-chosen poetry, also has the power for some to penetrate the barrier of grief and open up the bereaved to future possibilities. For all the positive comments received about the services conducted in church and the support given through the church, the brief poems, best shared in association with the Committal tend to have a special place in lifting spirits and providing comfort.

Three of these used on a number of occasions are shared below, but the ubiquitous Google has a whole section variously described as Poems For Funerals.

DEATH IS NOTHING AT ALL

Death is nothing at all.
It does not count.
I have only slipped away into the next room.
Nothing has happened.
Everything remains exactly as it was.
I am I, and you are you, and the old life that we lived so fondly together is untouched, unchanged.
Whatever we were to each other, that we are still.
Call me by the old familiar name.
Speak of me in the easy way which you always used.
Put no difference into your tone.
Wear no forced air of solemnity or sorrow.
Laugh as we always laughed at the little jokes that we enjoyed together. Play, smile, think of me, pray for me.
Let my name be ever the household word that it always was.
Let it be spoken without an effort, without the ghost of a shadow upon it. Life means all that it ever meant.
It is the same as it ever was.
There is absolute and unbroken continuity.
What is this death but a negligible accident
Why should I be out of mind because I am out of sight
I am but waiting for you, for an interval, somewhere very near, just round the corner.
All is well.
Nothing is hurt; nothing is lost.
One brief moment and all will be as it was before.
How we shall laugh at the trouble of parting when we meet again!

Henry Scott Holland (1847–1918)

IF I SHOULD DIE

If I should die before the rest of you
Break not a flower nor inscribe a stone
Nor, when I'm gone, speak in a Sunday voice.
But be the usual selves that I have known.
Weep if you must.
Parting is hell.
But life goes on.
So sing as well.

Joyce Grenfell (1910-1979)

SHE IS GONE (HE IS GONE)

You can shed tears that she is gone
Or you can smile because she has lived.
You can close your eyes and pray that she will come back
Or you can open your eyes and see all that she has left.
Your heart can be empty because you can't see her
Or you can be full of the love that you shared.
You can turn your back on tomorrow and live yesterday
Or you can be happy for tomorrow because of yesterday.
You can remember her and only that she is gone
Or you can cherish her memory and let it live on.
You can cry and close your mind, be empty and turn your back
Or you can do what she would want: smile, open your eyes, love and go on.

David Harkins

POSTSCRIPT: A PERSONAL TESTIMONY

When researching the material for this book, I came across a series of five brief morning talks on the subject of death that I gave on Radio Bristol from the 24th to the 28th October 1983. It did not seem inappropriate for the final pages of this book to include this very personal testimony that has helped mould my ministry to the bereaved for more than fifty years.

DEATH ---THE LAST THING WE TALK ABOUT

DAY ONE:

Good morning! Funny thing you know, but there never seems to be a right time to talk about death. Early morning hardly seems appropriate. But then, is the last thing at night? Not only is it never the right time of the day to talk about death, it never seems to be the right time in our lives.

The question "Have you made a will?" brings smiles to the faces of young couples who come to me for marriage counselling and provokes a negative reaction when asked in groups of older people.

Yet, if my experience is anything to go by, a great deal of upset, inconvenience and even financial loss can be incurred by a family when the person who has died didn't get round to making a will. All of us have to cope with the death of those near and dear to us, but, as the title of one book on death shrewdly observes, death is "The Last Thing We talk About."

At this time over the next few days, we shall be talking about death and our human reaction to the death of someone we have loved.

If what I say does no more than encourage you to talk more openly and honestly to others about death, I shall have achieved my purpose.

DAY TWO:

Good morning! This week we are talking about our human reaction to death. For some people the hatching, matching and dispatching columns of the daily newspaper are obligatory reading: there we can look with interest at those who have had babies, those who have married, and those who have died. We are observers rather than participants in the drama of life. How different is our response when we are drawn into the drama by the death of someone we have loved?

C. S. Lewis, a Christian writer of serious books as well as children's stories, in a book entitled 'A Grief Observed', describes his reactions to his wife's death after a long and painful illness.

We can identify with his initial reaction as a sense of bewilderment,

The shock of death brings with it a sense of unreality to those who are left behind - a feeling that it cannot really have happened, a desire to replay the video and have a different ending.

Death has suddenly become personal. Our great need at this time is not conversation to take our minds off it but companionship to help us through it.

For several years I worked in Sierra Leone in West Africa.

When someone died in the village a whole procession of people would visit the home just to sit with the bereaved.

Friends showed they cared and they brought the family comfort, simply by being there.

Perhaps this is a lesson that we could learn.

DAY THREE:

Good morning! We heard yesterday how the shock of someone's death can send us into a trance-like state of unreality, almost as though we have been drugged.

The pain that follows as we begin again to face reality is like that which we feel on waking up from an operation. The sharp pain has gone but the dull ache is still there and the questions begin to flow.

Whether or not we claim to believe in God, the questions that follow from the death of someone we have loved become religious questions about the meaning of life.

Like Job in the Old Testament, we challenge God to justify himself. Unlike Job the only reply we seem to get to the question "Why?" feels in the words of C. S. Lewis, like a door slammed in your face.

Now, in the midst of grief is not the time for an academic discussion on the problem of suffering or the meaning of life. This is the time to hold on to the familiar in daily life and take comfort from worship and the tradition of your own religion.

It's at such times that Christians receive comfort from the words of the 23rd Psalm beginning,

"The Lord's my shepherd, I shall not want,"

and from the words of Jesus in John's Gospel Chapter 14

"Let not your hearts be troubled; believe in God, believe also in me. In my father's house are many rooms."

Peace I leave with you; my peace I give to you."

DAY FOUR:

Good morning! In coping with grief after a bereavement we can be helped through the immediate shock by sympathetic and sensitive friends and through the emotional and spiritual pain that follows by clinging to the familiar in life and religion.

We are all different and must do what seems right for us during the early stages of grief.

In doing this, we will discover that a further obstacle to our acceptance of death and recovery from grief is guilt. Feelings of guilt so often accompany the death of a loved one.

Guilt for things said or done to the one who has died that we wish we could undo.

Guilt for parents not visited or thanks never expressed.

Guilt about our reactions to death or doubting of God.

Guilt when we begin to sleep through the night again, when a sunny morning brings a smile to our face or a humorous situation brings laughter to our lips,

"Have you so soon forgotten?" the nagging voice of guilt says.
Often the guilt feelings are reinforced by thoughtless people who know what we ought to do or how we ought to behave and by our own inner doubts about what others expect of us. In dealing with guilt, we need to learn how to forgive ourselves as well as other people in the confessional of our own hearts and churches.

Guilt is too big a burden to carry round for the rest of your life.

DAY FIVE:

Good morning! This week we have been talking about our natural human reaction to death and grief and the way to a complete recovery.

Let me re-trace the steps again out of my own experience.

Less than twelve months after I had entered theological college to train for the Methodist ministry, I was told that my mother was dying of cancer and had less than two months to live.

The shock of her death brought life to a standstill for me – it could not really have happened-but it had.

The spiritual and emotional pain followed, as I questioned God's love and his failure to answer my prayers.

The guilt feelings about how little I had done to help her mocked my Christian calling to the ministry,

It took time for these questions to be worked through, but almost imperceptibly God came back into focus.

As one who loves enough to give his children freedom.
As one whose purposes are measured by eternity.
As one who brings order into the chaos of life and human experience.

In talking about death, we are challenged to think about life and its relation to eternity.

For me, Jesus Christ is the one who gives meaning to life and makes sense of death.

Deciding what they believe about death has helped many people and may help you, to a fresh understanding of what matters in life.

Lightning Source UK Ltd.
Milton Keynes UK
UKHW012107290721
387926UK00001B/46